Utopian Literature

Advisory Editor:
ARTHUR ORCUTT LEWIS, JR.
    Professor of English
The Pennsylvania State University

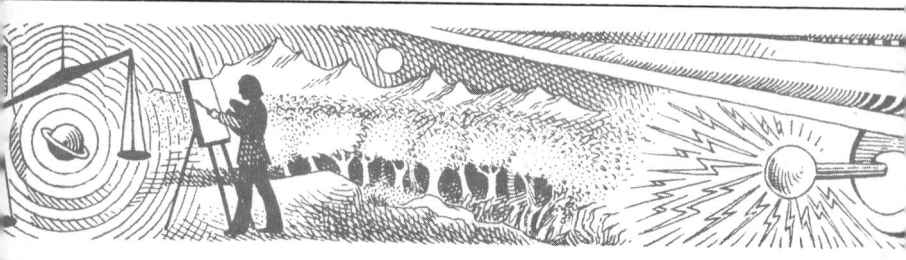

The Future Commonwealth

Albert Chavannes

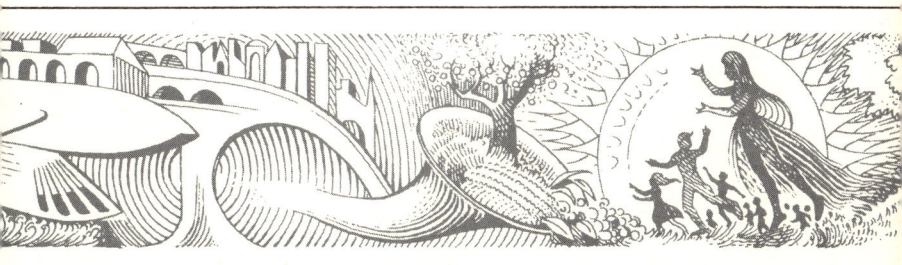

ARNO PRESS & THE NEW YORK TIMES
NEW YORK · 1971

Reprint Edition 1971 by Arno Press Inc.

Reprinted from a copy in The Pennsylvania State University Library

LC# 71-154433
ISBN 0-405-03516-0

Utopian Literature
ISBN for complete set: 0-405-03510-1

Manufactured in the United States of America

Publisher's Note: This edition was reprinted from the best available copy

THE FUTURE COMMONWEALTH,

OR

WHAT SAMUEL BALCOM SAW IN SOCIOLAND.

BY

ALBERT CHAVANNES.

[Copyright secured.]

NEW YORK:
TRUE NATIONALIST PUBLISHING COMPANY.
1892.

CONTENTS.

			Page.
Chapter	1.	The Exodus,	1
"	2.	The Object in View,	6
"	3.	Some Reflections,	15
"	4.	A Philosophical Digression,	19
"	5.	The Changes Made,	26
"	6.	At The Hotel,	33
"	7.	Public Management,	40
"	8.	The Right Spirit,	47
"	9.	The Apprentices,	53
"	10.	About Education,	60
"	11.	Ancient Institutions,	67
"	12.	Housekeeping in Socioland,	73
"	13.	A True Commonwealth,	80
"	14.	A Pleasant Ride,	87
"	15.	The Land Question,	94
"	16.	Arbitration and Laws,	101
"	17.	The Conditions of Success,	108

EXPLANATORY.

In presenting the following pages to the public, I desire to say a few words to explain the motives which have led to their publication. This can best be done by first quoting a few sentences from an address upon the Problems of our Second Century, delivered by Ex-Senator Ingalls at Glen-Echo in the summer of 1891.

Speaking of the evil results of our present industrial system, Mr. Ingalls said: "From 1860 to 1890 the country has grown richer at the rate of 250,000 dollars for every day and hour of these thirty years. There has been accumulated during that term one hundred thousand millions of dollars, enough to give every man, woman and child beneath the flag a competency, enough to secure to every family a comfortable home, to educate and keep the wolf from every door, and to guard against every misfortune and calamity.

"And yet," he continued with a dramatic uplifting of his hands, "there are ten millions of people out of sixty-five millions that never get enough to eat from one year's end to the other."

The speaker presented a strong contrast between the laborer working incessantly, only to end his life in helpless mendicity, and the 31,000 persons who hold more than one half of the acquired earnings for the last hundred years. With a scathing denunciation of the extravagance which spends 10,000 dollars on flowers for a wedding, and repeating that 31,000 men controlled one half of the wealth of the country, Mr. Ingalls strolled to the front of the platform, and raising his slender form to its full height, exclaimed: "If thirty thousand men can do this, what is to prevent one man from getting control of all?

"The doctrine of 'the devil takes the hindmost'," continued

EXPLANATORY.

Mr. Ingalls, "is a good one, but just now it seems as if there were more hindmost than foremost. If the present condition of things were to continue without being retarded, this land, instead of being the land of the free and the home of the brave, would be the land of the rich and the home of the slave."

Making due allowance for the exaggeration of an impulsive speaker, there is enough truth in Mr. Ingalls' indictment to explain the general dissatisfaction which now exists with the results of our present economic system.

Mr. Ingalls does not believe in the efficiency of the remedies offered by the Nationalists, and he presented his objections in a very forcible manner.

"There is," he said, "a growing sentiment in favor of Paternalism in this country—of the government doing everything—of the people doing nothing. We have now a new school of political philosophy that is repudiating the declaration of independence and is endeavoring to overthrow the maxims of democracy and to insist that the race shall not be to the strong, that the distinctions ordained of God shall be an obliterated statute, that idleness shall bring the same reward as industry and thrift, that the ignorant shall be as wise as the learned, that debts shall be paid by acts of Congress, that money shall be made as plenty as the autumn leaves, that taxation shall be abolished by acts of the Legislature, and that property shall be forcibly distributed among men."

It is to answer just such objections that this story has been written, for they are often heard among practical men who have really the welfare of the community at heart. These objections cannot be answered in a few words, and it has seemed to me that it could best be done by portraying a Commonwealth where the changes we advocate have already been accomplished, showing how the desired results can be attained

EXPLANATORY.

without resorting to such revolutionary methods as would never meet with the approval of sensible and practical men, and that without passing the limits of the possible and practicable, many changes could be made that would cause great improvement.

For in this picture of a Future Commonwealth I have not drawn on my imagination, but I have carefully studied the line which progress has followed since the dawn of civilization, and have endeavored to portray the changes which will probably take place in the course of coming years.

If my readers will take the trouble to investigate, they will find that what I have described as being part of the public institutions of Socioland, already exists in its incipient stages in one or the other of the civilized nations. And furthermore they will find that the tendency to progress in the direction described manifests itself now in a greater degree than it did one or two hundred years ago.

Many of these tendencies, it is true, are not yet strong enough to affect the laws or public institutions, but their influence is felt among the most intelligent part of the population, that is, among those who lead in the march of progress.

As some objections have been made, during the publication of this story in serial form, in the *True Nationalist*, both as to the philosophical belief and to the spirit which controls the enactment of the laws in Socioland, it seems well to me to say a few words in explanation.

The reaction of all changes upon the surroundings is now recognized as a positive fact. We realize now that the success of one nation affects more or less all other nations, and that a change in one country implies a corresponding change in all other countries.

But too many students of social science fail to understand

that the same law holds good in the social relations, and we now have the spectacle of a world full of social reformers who, dissatisfied with some of the present conditions, strive with main and might to change them, and at the same time strive just as hard to prevent corresponding changes in other directions. With one hand they push along the car of progress and with the other they work just as hard to hold it back.

Nothing, in my estimation, has more influence upon progress, aside from the motive power furnished by the desire for increased happiness, than the religious beliefs of the people. They control its conduct, public and private, and are responsible for the spirit of its laws.

Increased knowledge has opened to mankind greater prospects of happiness, which have been checked by religious beliefs handed down to us by past generations.

The result is that our religion and our environment no longer agree. The environment is of to-day, the religion is of the past.

This is felt and realized by all those who earnestly study the social problems, and strenuous efforts are made to shape and trim the old religious doctrines so as to make them fit the new social conditions.

At the rate this work is progressing, it will not be a great many years before the spirit of the Christian religion will have been entirely changed; and according to the changes which have already taken place within the church, supplemented by the beliefs which are growing in favor outside the church, I think I am justified in claiming that sometime in the near future, religion will resolve itself in something like the philosophical beliefs expressed by Mr. Walter in the third Chapter of this story.

The influence of the religious beliefs upon laws and conduct has led me to devote some space to the subject, for I claim that our economic condition is the logical outcome of our present religious belief, and that both must change together if any progress is achieved.

In the sixteenth Chapter, I have, very briefly and inadequately, tried to express my views as to the spirit which will animate the coming generations and control the enactment of their laws.

Every thinking person must acknowledge that nations are growing more sympathetic and less quarrelsome, and that a spirit of leniency is replacing the "eye for an eye and tooth for a tooth" doctrine of olden times. In proof thereof I can point to the exemption clauses in the laws for the collection of debts, and the growing tendency to compel arbitration in cases of disputes between employers and their laborers. Both exemption and enforced arbitration are steps away from exact justice and natural rights, and are the result of a sympathetic desire to help those who are defeated in the battle of life.

It is true that the American people, as a nation, have as much faith as ever in the efficacy of the law as a moral regulator, but among their best men the feeling is growing that people cannot be made moral by law, and other nations have progressed beyond us in this direction.

I have not touched upon the population question, and have said but a word about the marriage relation, not because I do not recognize their importance in the solution of the social problems, but because they are not as fundamental as the question of religious beliefs.

Yet I wish to put myself on record here as believing that the tendency of the times is toward educating the individuals so as to enable them to fulfil their duties as citizens in a satisfactory manner without the need of state control, and that the coming generations will be able to allow individuals much more freedom in their personal actions.

EXPLANATORY.

Nationalism, in fact, will only prove acceptable in so far as it will know how to reconcile economic organization with personal liberty.

I not only believe that it can be done, but I feel confident that it will be done; and that it will come to pass in the evolution of social progress, that wrangling, competing humanity as we know it to-day, will, in its persistent search after increased happiness, organize itself into true Commonwealths, with institutions somewhat like those I have tried to picture as existing in Socioland.

How long will it take before it comes to pass? How far will the work of organization progress? are questions the future alone can answer.

For the present I shall be satisfied if I succeed in convincing some inquiring mind that Nationalism is not an impossible dream, and that it offers prospects of improvement for society, which are well worth the consideration of intelligent citizens.

Albert Chavannes.
Knoxville, Tenn.

THE
FUTURE COMMONWEALTH

CHAPTER I.

THE EXODUS.

Spencer, Socioland, Africa,
June 1, 1950.

My dear friend Harry :

I have at last reached this place after a long and interesting journey, and I will at once commence a journal, which when complete, will enable me to fulfil my promise that I would try to faithfully report to you whatever I should see or hear which could throw any light upon the social problems in which we are both interested.

I have no doubt, from what I have seen of the people since I entered the Commonwealth of Socioland, that if I do not find here a complete solution of the problems which perplex us, I will find at least the results of interesting experiments in Sociology, and valuable hints as to the best course to be followed to secure a better distribution of wealth, and an increase of general comfort.

For I must at once acknowledge that these people seem much better satisfied than we are, and while they recognize that they have not yet attained perfect social conditions, still they are confident that they are travelling in the right direction, and that all desirable changes will come easily and naturally in the course of time.

But before I enter upon a detailed account of what I see and hear, I want to tell you of the causes which led to the settlement of Socioland, as well as of the aims of the first emigrants, which controlled their conduct and form the basis of their public and private institutions.

I am enabled to do so from information I received from Mr. Walter, an old gentleman whom I found on the boat, a native of Ohio, who nearly fifty years ago emigrated to this country, and I judge from his conversation, took an active part in shaping the policy of the Commonwealth.

You know as well as I do that the latter end of the XIXth century was a time of great changes. Not only of a great development of the natural resources and of the producing power of mankind through the increased use of steam and of electricity, but also of changes in the religious, scientific and philosophical beliefs of the educated classes.

It was then that through the researches of Darwin, Spencer and others, commenced that period of religious doubt in which we still are in the United States. Truly before their time there had been skeptics and railers at the Christian religion, men and women who denied the authority of the Bible, but their number was small, their influence null, and civilized society was willing yet to be controlled by persons who either believed, or claimed to believe, that the ten commandments were the expression of the will of God, and that the more closely they could be followed and enforced, the better the results would be. These persons explained the suffering and misery of the masses as due to the innate depravity of human nature, and the poor were kept quiet by alternate doses of charity and of promises of eternal bliss in the world to come.

The doctrine of evolution, taught and accepted towards the

end of the century, sapped this belief at its basis, and it was soon recognized by those who undertook to follow it to its logical conclusions that the whole philosophy of the past, built upon a belief in special creation, would have to be remodeled until an entire change had been effected in religious beliefs, and that eventually the social institutions themselves would be thereby influenced.

The spread of these doctrines among persons of progressive minds caused naturally a great commotion, and for a long time confusion worse confounded was the result. According to Mr. Walter these years were the scene of such intellectual wrangling as the world had never seen or will probably ever see again. First came the believers in these new teachings, enthusiastically fighting for the acceptance of what they considered the truth, and thus ruthlessly tearing down the foundations of the Christian beliefs, who were met and opposed by those who, honestly or from interested motives, clung to Christianity, and resisted all attacks which threatened its existence; while mixing in the din of the battle were a legion of persons, each with a patent remedy of his own for all the ills of society, striving for recognition, and trying by all means in their power to bring their schemes before the public while the masses, fast losing their interest in things spiritual and their fear of damnation, and more interested in physical comforts than in speculations of a philosophical nature, turned, their attention to the practical work of developing the natural resources opened to them through the increase of mechanical forces, and the extension of the means of communication.

Out of this intellectual struggle soon emerged here and there practical men and women who, discarding religious speculations as to a future existence, and the Bible as a guide for their actions, studied the laws of conduct in a scientific spirit, and with the firm intention to profit by any

4   THE FUTURE COMMONWEALTH.

new truths they might discover. These persons, scattered in every part of the United States, were soon drawn together by a common aim, and under the name of Sociologists, or students of Social Science, formed themselves into clubs for the pursuit of social knowledge, and to seek for means of practical application of such knowledge as could help them to a more satisfactory mode of life and a better form of government.

In the pursuit of new knowledge they claim to have been entirely successful, and to have discovered many new social laws which, if applied, would greatly benefit society. But when they tried to give their new knowledge practical force, they found it a more difficult task than they had anticipated. The number of persons interested in such studies as they pursued was comparatively very small, and the whole control of the government was in the hands of men who had a direct interest in opposing any changes and were entrenched behind centuries of possession. The masses were too indifferent or ignorant to offer a fair hope of awakening to a better way out of their misery, and personal conduct was yet largely controlled by laws enacted by men who were earnest believers in the infallibility of the Bible, and who felt it their duty to compel by force those who might disagree with them.

It is not strange that out of such conditions grew an earnest desire to seek by emigration a land where their new ideas could find free development in a virgin and unoccupied country, and that like the Pilgrim Fathers, earnest men and women should decide to leave home, friends and relations, in the endeavor to found a settlement where they would be free to follow the dictates of their intelligence.

The opening of the Dark Continent furnished them with the desired opportunity. Several European powers had established protectorates over large and unsettled portions of the country, and were anxious to see them inhabited by a population which could help to check the slave trade, and open new outlets to commerce.

Taking advantage of this situation, trusty men were selected to spy the country and see what prospect it offered. They were remarkably successful, found a large valley with fertile soil and healthy climate, and capable of supporting a large population. They made a treaty with the protecting power which guaranteed to the proposed settlement complete autonomy in their internal government, and they were assured of protection against foreign foes so long as they could not protect themselves.

In the mean time the home clubs had made ready for the coming immigration as soon as the way should be open, and a comparatively large and steady exodus took place from the United States to the land of promise which they baptized with the name of Socioland.

Of course they had many difficulties to contend with, but now they have overcome them and they are a prosperous and happy people. Their prosperity and happiness is not the result of chance or of special advantages pertaining to their new country. It is due to the fact that their conduct, public and private, is intelligently controlled by what they claim to be scientific principles. They believe in a social science, which they claim is something different from political economy. They study this science, and instead of allowing the doctrine of *Laissez faire* full sway, and trusting to natural forces alone to remedy existing evils, they are not afraid to help nature along, and to experiment in new lines of public co-operation whenever they seem to lead in the right direction.

So much it was necessary for me to say, to explain to you how it came to pass that in this far off land, a settlement of our countrymen has been made, embued with entirely different ideas from those which obtain in Europe and America.

Just as New England was settled by earnest men and women, having special aims and profound convictions, who infused a new country and a new nation with a new spirit, which has stamped its mark upon the United States government and upon the character of the people, so in this land a new spirit has been infused, which, according to my information, has produced wonderful results.

Of this, however, we can judge better when I have mixed more with the people, and I am better acquainted with the institutions which they have here inaugurated.

CHAPTER II.

THE OBJECT IN VIEW.

I found Mr Walter a very pleasant companion, and during the few days we spent together I received from him much valuable information. When from questions I made to him he understood why I was going to Socioland, and learned from my lips of the deep interest I felt in social problems, he seemed as desirous of imparting knowledge as I was to receive it, and tried to facilitate by all means in his power the aims I had in view.

"Mr. Balcom," he said to me one evening as we were sitting in the cabin conversing upon Socioland, "it will help you very much to understand what you will see in our country if you know the object we had in view in coming here, as well as some of the means by which we expected to attain it.

"There has been, as you know, many an exodus before our own, but I believe they were all actuated by very different motives from those which induced us to leave our native land. The Hebrews were fleeing from bondage, the Puritans were trying to escape religious persecution, and the Mormons wanted to establish a religious hierarchy. On a smaller scale, but under similar influences, many communities and co-operative colonies have been started, but they all had a definite plan which they wanted to work out. We had no settled plan, no definite scheme, but we had a very clear idea of the results we were going to strive for.

" We were dissatisfied with society as organized in the United States, and did not believe that it afforded to the individual all the facilities for comfort and happiness which the natural advantages warranted.

"With the increase of population and wealth many abuses had been fostered that we felt powerless to remedy, and a spirit of greed, strife and competition had been engendered which was uncongenial to our character. Besides we had outgrown the old ideas of religious morality, and were tired of having our personal actions under the control of laws enacted by men whose standard of morals was not based upon the result of our conduct on our happiness, but upon certain commandments and precepts which may have been proper enough in the barbarous times in which they were promulgated, but had become superannuated several centuries ago.

"These causes of dissatisfaction affected not us alone, but the conservative influences were yet so strong that improvement was very slow, and we preferred to go to a new country where we would be free to live according to our own ideas of right.

"We had faith in the good disposition of human nature, and believed that, if rightly taught, all persons would recognize that whatever promoted the general welfare would also promote personal happiness. We wanted to educate our people to the recognition of the solidarity of the interests of the human race, and by this knowledge replace as far as possible the checks to selfish greed. now restrained, but not diminished, by religious authority and human law.

"But, Mr. Balcom, we were not reformers according to the meaning of the word among you. We had no patent remedy warranted to cure all the ills that the flesh is heir to. We did not claim to know everything, and we were fully aware that we could not lay down any positive rule of conduct as best for us to follow. We were dissatisfied with existing conditions, and wanted to see what desirable changes we could make. We had no desire to overturn the existing conditions of society, or to give up anything which then gave satisfaction. We wanted to try to improve the public institutions a little faster than was possible with the ideas prevailing in the United States, and to conform our conduct to the laws of nature, and thus increase our prospects of earthly happiness.

"As you can see our aims were very broad, for it was not one special evil we wanted to correct, but we wanted a general improvement, based upon a radical change in the foundations of the aims and beliefs which control society.

"The broadness of our aims was a great help to the success of our experiment. Our object being the attainment of happiness, all efforts which resulted in its increase were welcomed, and no fault found with the means employed. Our submission to nature's laws made us submissive to nature's methods, and we could but approve of what nature rewarded.

"In a word, we applied to social science the same tests that are universally applied to chemistry, mechanics, or any other exact science. If any one claims to have discovered some chemical formula, or mechanical combination, which gives satisfactory results, all he has to do is to prove it by practical experiments, and if successful it is adopted by general consent.

But in your country you have no test to apply to social experiments, for you have no social science worthy of the name, and the best results would be either ignored or denounced, if brought about by means opposed to the commandments of Moses or the teachings of Jesus.

"We believed then, and we believe now, that a righteous end sanctifies the means, and not as is taught among you that righteous means sanctify the end. And we further believe that, so far as man is concerned, an increase of his earthly happiness is a righteous end, approved of by the laws of nature, and that all means which tend to accomplish that result are right and proper.

"And it is because we Sociologists have accepted the increase of happiness as legitimate pursuit, encouraged and rewarded by the laws of nature, and have accepted the achievement of happiness as a correct standard for public and private actions, that we decided to leave home, family, and friends, and establish a new Commonwealth where greed, strife, and competition would be held at a discount, and peace and happiness fostered."

Mr. Walter paused a moment, for our conversation had taken him back to the days of his youth and to the memories of the past. But not for long, for fixing his earnest grey eyes on me he contiuued: "Mr Balcom, when you reach Socioland you will find yourself in a new atmosphere. Remember what I am telling you, for it will help you to understand how we have succeeded to accomplish many difficult undertakings. The desire for happiness brings many valuable results in its train. It fosters peace, leads to kindness, encourages unity. It teaches the value of health and comfort. It softens the heart and broadens the sympathies. Seekers after happiness cultivate their minds and exercise all their faculties. Yes, the pursuit of happiness is a wonderful civilizing influence. I have watched it at work for fifty years and more, and it has accomplished greater results than centuries of fear or of promises of eternal bliss.

"You can have no idea what a help it has been to us in the first years we spent here, when the many different opinions which must naturally manifest themselves at the beginning of such an enterprise might have divided us in many factions. But instead of each insisting on the special merit of his scheme, we were all willing to submit to the test of practical experience, and were also decided to remain united whatever might happen, for we believed that the friendship of our associates was more conducive to our happiness than the adoption of some pet opinion of ours. And now that we have safely launched our social bark, and have achieved satisfactory results, we are more united than ever."

I was very much interested in Mr. Walter's statement, and in the earnestness of his convictions, and as he paused I remarked to him that I thought he had given me a clearer idea of the object they had in view, and that I wanted him to tell me how they went to work to reorganize society.

"But do you not understand," he replied, "that we did not intend to reorganize society. We wanted to improve it. We did not believe in setting aside all the past experience of mankind, and reconstructing society on entirely new lines. We wanted to improve it on the same old lines, which is a very different thing. New conditions had created new abuses, and we wanted to stop them as far as possible. Not only did we want to feel free to work out our own happiness in our own way, but we could see also that while the United States produced plentifully, the distribution was very defective."

"You are entirely right," I remarked, "and probably more dissatisfaction is felt among us on account of the inequality in the distribution of wealth than from any other cause."

THE OBJECT IN VIEW. 11

"It is natural that it should be so," continued Mr. Walter, "for while production is not as large as it might or will eventually be, still it is large enough to keep every one in comfort if it was rightly distributed, and it is a crying shame that in this advanced age of ours, some should be rolling in wealth, while others are shivering and starving.

"We consider the distribution of products as the most important question placed before civilized communities, and that its correct solution offers the best prospect of increasing the sum total of human happiness. From our standpoint, unequal distribution is a two-edged sword which cuts both ways. On one side you have the wealthy class, which lives in idleness, their wants supplied by hirelings, having no aim in life except to pass the time which before middle age drags heavily on their hands, while all around them lives another class, unable to secure a little of the leisure and some of the luxuries which prevent the exercise of the most valuable faculties of their more wealthy but not more happy neighbors.

"Nor are the relations between the two classes satisfactory. The sympathies of the rich are wounded by the sight of the privations of the poor, while the poor see with more and more envious eyes the ever increasing possessions of the rich. Thus the relations between the rich and the poor become more strained, and in a measure the steady increase of production tends to diminish instead of increasing the happiness of mankind."

"You need not enlarge upon this theme, Mr. Walter," I replied. "You cannot frame a stronger indictment against the evil effects of our system of distribution than you will hear at any time in the United States. All who study the social problems realize the evil, for it is much worse now than it was at the time you left our country. The rich have grown in number and wealth and are drawing everything into their hands, while the poor, growing more intelligent and better educated, realize more and more that they do not receive the full reward of their labors.

"But what can we do about it? Where is the remedy? We cannot despoil the rich for the benefit of the poor, for it would destroy the accumulation of capital and diminish production. The diffusion of capital in the hands of so many untrained and incompetent persons would soon destroy it, and the final result would be the impoverishment of the whole country without any improvement in the condition of the poor."

"Very true," answered Mr. Walter. "It is a difficult question, but I can tell you what we have done, and how we have succeeded in keeping down this inequality between the classes, and prevented the acquisition of the lion's share of the produced wealth by a few privileged members of society.

"But let me remind you of one thing. It is not because we believe in perfect equality, or that all men are entitled to an equal share of the production, that we object to the wide distinction which now exists between the opulent rich and the abject poor. It is because the rich have more than they can enjoy, while the poor have less, that we believe a better system of distribution will benefit all. This very much simplifies the problem, for if we can find the source of excessive wealth, and turn it into a reservoir for the benefit of all classes, our aim will be practically attained.

"And that is what we have done. The large accumulation of wealth in private hands is not the result of the toil of these persons, for no man can by daily labor accumulate more than will insure him a comfortable living. Excessive private wealth is the result of social causes which encourage and reward the cumulative power of capital.

"No, we knew well enough that the diffusion of capital leads to its destruction, and that all means which would tend to its equal distribution would result in a diminution of production and a reduction of general comfort.

"So the measures we took led in an entirely different direction. We made our new Commonwealth the great Capitalist, and thus as far as possible prevented the undue accumulation of wealth in private hands.

"There, Mr. Balcom, is the whole secret of it. Co-operation on a large scale, not practised by a few, for the advantage of a few, as it exists among you, but carried by the Commonwealth, for the advantage of the whole population, for the rich as well as for the poor, for the women as well as for the men."

I must confess I was somewhat disappointed, for it was nothing new for me to hear such doctrines, and I exclaimed: "Oh! then your Socioland is simply a Socialistic settlement, where the state controls everything. It may suit you, but I doubt if it would suit me or many of the free and independent citizens of America."

A malicious twinkle gleamed in Mr. Walter's eyes.

"Free and independent indeed! Then things have wonderfully changed since my time. When I lived in the United States, in the days of my youth, I recollect hearing a great deal about the slavery of labor, and freedom in trade with foreign countries was unknown. We had Sunday laws regulating the use of the days, and marriage and divorce laws controlling private associations. Prohibitive laws on liquor were in force in many states, while to crown this free social edifice, the Mormon persecution was in all its glory.

"Reassure yourself, we have not abridged personal liberty as much as you have, and are not Socialists as you understand the term. All governments are somewhat Socialists, some a little more, others a little less. We are a little more, and have intrusted the Commonwealth with the accumulation and use of a portion of our capital for the benefit of our people, while you only intrust your government with the spending of such capital as you raise by unequal taxation, or by borrowing from the wealthy class, thus increasing the burdens of the producers by compelling them to pay the interest on the money your government spends.

"Do you sometimes reflect, Mr. Balcom, how the different enterprises, created by the growing needs of our civilization, are divided in the United States? Take the cities for instance. Whatever costs money to maintain, as the streets and the parks, the police and the fire department, etc., is placed in the hands of the government, and the people are taxed for its support, while those enterprises which offer opportunities to make money, as the supply of light and water, the life and fire insurances, are allowed to fall into the hands of corporations and individuals.

"We are so far Socialists as to claim that the sweet ought to go with the sour, and to keep in the possession of the people many valuable privileges which you give away to men who use them for their private benefit.

"But," pulling out his watch, "I see it is getting late, and we had better retire. To-morrow we will find plenty of time to talk before we reach Spencer, and I will explain to you at length the changes we inaugurated in the public institutions of Socioland."

CHAPTER III.

SOME REFLECTIONS.

I believe, my dear Harry, that what I will see and hear in this country will keep my mind busy, and that I will have many new ideas to digest. I can see already that their way of looking at the social problems is entirely different from ours. They look them square in the face, with a clear conception of the ends they are striving for, and do not allow themselves to stray hither and thither after false issues as we are inclined to do.

Mr. Walter was emphatic, and his whole manner expressive of quiet determination, and he succeeded in giving me a clear impression of the aims and methods of the people of Socioland.

After I had gone to rest it was a long time before I could go to sleep. That which had struck me the most in our conversation was Mr. Walter's frank avowal that as a people they were engaged in the pursuit of happiness. There was no false pretense of trying to serve the Lord, no claim of helping to promote morality, no holding aloof a beacon for the benefit of other nations.

Instead, these people freely acknowledged that they were experimenting for themselves, trying to increase their own happiness, owing no allegiance except to the laws of nature, recognizing no duty except that of improving their faculties and making the most of existing conditions.

That was something entirely new in my experience. I had, of course, come across young people with more money than brains, who said they wanted a good time, and were going to enjoy all the pleasure that this life can afford, but among the sensible, respectable people of my acquaintance, the pursuit of happiness was looked down upon as a low standard of life, leading to selfishness, and degrading in its tendencies.

To be sure I could not tell what was the aim in life of these respectable acquaintances of mine. Had I asked them, which I never thought of doing, I would probably have found they did not know themselves. I knew the religious teachings on that subject, and that we are admonished to so live as to glorify God. But my friends did not believe any such doctrines, or if they believed them, they made no pretense to put them in practice in their daily life, being of the kind who give their religion a Sunday airing, putting it carefully away during the week to preserve it from unseemly wear, so as to have it bright and shining on the rare occasions they are called upon to parade it before the world.

As my mind roamed over the list of my acquaintances, I could think of Mr. B., whose whole ambition seemed to be to make money, of which he had already more than himself or his family could use. His wife was a society leader, and her object in life was to outshine her rivals. His sons were certainly bent on pleasure, but with their expensive habits, effeminate tastes, and shattered constitutions, were not happy, and were positive proof of the fact that the pursuit of happiness and of pleasure are entirely different.

And our neighbor D., is he living for happiness? If he is, he seems to make a miserable failure of it. An overworked, tired-out man, without a minute he can call his own, following an incessant round of occupations which have no interest for him, he is kept constantly tramping in a commercial treadmill for a bare support for himself and his large family. His wife, whom I can remember as the lively, sweet Alice T., is now a tired, dissatisfied woman. That couple had probably in the early days of their marriage anticipated a happy life, but the result had not come up to their fond expectations.

From them my thoughts turned to the contemplation of myself. What was I living for? I really could not answer. An Agnostic, I was not living in view of a future life, and yet I realized that I was certainly not studying how to attain the highest satisfaction possible in this world.

As I reflected, I could see very clearly that I had no definite standard of conduct, and that the principles which controlled my life were of a very composite nature. Raised outside the church, by parents who had outgrown the Christian beliefs without accepting any other, my moral education had been desultory in the extreme. At one time my father railed at the Christian dogmas, or made fun of their puritanical ideas and sanctimonious ways. At other times he would impress upon me the beauty of the Christian doctrine of self-renunciation, quote the golden rule, and call Christ the greatest teacher that ever lived. Again he would preach the doctrine of duty, how we must respect our parents, obey the laws, help our neighbors, work for humanity. But these moods did not last always. I was also taught that I must learn to take care of number one, fight for standing room, and strike out for myself if I would not be crushed.

Out of such teachings the usual results had followed. I simply drifted, one day following the voice of duty, and the next allowing the care of self to predominate. The outcome was not very satisfactory, but I could not see my way to anything better, and I consoled myself with the thought that I was doing about as well as the average of those by whom I was surrounded.

Now that my attention was called to it, I could see that instead of having a well-defined aim in life, and controlling my conduct in the manner best calculated to attain it, I allowed myself to be swayed by the ideas, beliefs and habits of the people among whom I lived, who themselves had no accurate knowledge of right or wrong, but were following blindly in the footsteps of their superstitious ancestors.

Mr. Walter's conversation made a profound impression upon me, for I was logical enough to see that our conduct in life must be largely controlled by the character of the solution we accept for the problem of existence, and if practically concurred in by a whole people, it must have a great influence on their public institutions. A nation with divided or indefinite aims would drift along, where one with clear and decided opinions would adopt efficient means to insure success.

As is the seed, so must the tree be, and if the people of Socioland are happier and more contented than the people of the United States, then I must conclude that they have the best institutions.

I cogitated over these things a long time, wondering if these people were really right, and if the pursuit of happiness is the only safe guide to conduct; and if the old barriers erected to restrain selfishness were thrown down, who would protect the weak from the strong, or settle the terms of compromise between individual happiness and public welfare when they came in conflict?

Worn out with thoughts, I decided to present these questions for solution to Mr. Walter the first thing in the morning, and after hearing what he has to say on the subject, to wait and see with my own eyes the working of these principles in Socioland. Theoretical ideas must give way before practical results. I would try and set aside all prejudice and pre-conceived beliefs, and impartially observe the life of the inhabitants of the Commonwealth.

Of one thing I am certain. There is a great deal of misery in this world, and even a slight increase of happiness is well worth striving for.

CHAPTER IV.

A PHILOSOPHICAL DIGRESSION.

The next morning I took the first opportunity to propound my questions to Mr. Walter. I told him that before he said any more about the social changes they had instituted, I wanted to have some explanations of their doctrine of accepting the attainment of happiness as a standard of conduct, and presented to him some of the objections which had arisen in my mind.

"My young friend," he answered, "I am glad to see that you appreciate the importance of this question. One of the first conditions of success is the concentration of our powers towards the object we wish to attain, which is only possible if we have a clear conception of what we wish to accomplish.

"If there is so little happiness in this world, it is largely due to the fact that not many of the efforts of men have been directed towards it.

"Some men seek for pleasure, others for wealth or fame, many are trying to serve God and Mammon, others are only anxious to secure eternal bliss, while all Christians, sincere or otherwise, are under the influence of teachings which deprecate the pursuit of earthly happiness as inimical to the will of God.

"We, on the other hand, believe in the pursuit of happiness just as the sincere Christian believes in serving the Lord. We believe that in so doing we are working in the line of progress, and that to attain it we must not only cultivate all the best there is in us, but that it will also induce us to adopt those public institutions best calculated to increase the welfare of society.

"I cannot explain to you why we believe those things except by indulging in a little philosophical talk, something that is not always interesting to the young. However, if you will kindly listen to what I want to say, I will try to be brief, and possibly you may be rewarded for your patience.

"We believe in evolution, in development, in latent potentiality. We believe that until the advent of man, development followed what we call the natural process, and that under this process, plants, animals, and men were evolved.

"But we further believe that when this natural process had finished its work, the latent potentiality of development was not yet exhausted, and that the way was just made ready for a further stage of development which we call artificial, —in contrast to the natural, although both are according to the laws of nature—which requires for its accomplishment a highly organized and intelligent agent.

"Man, who is the last and highest product of natural evolution, is this agent calculated to promote this artificial development, and is well fitted for the work by his ever-increasing consciousness and intelligence. Through consciousness he dreads pain and enjoys pleasant sensations, by intelligence he recognizes the nature of his surroundings, and learns how to control his conduct so as to escape the one and increase the other.

"The law of progress, as we understand it, is this: All those actions of men which tend to advance artificial development, —or civilization, to give it its popular name—produce at once, or ultimately through their complex results, pleasant sensations, and thus encourage men to repeat them; while all those actions of men which tend to obstruct civilization, produce at once, or ultimately by their complex results, unpleasant sensations, and thus discourage men from repeating them.

"'Under this law civilization has been carried and all the

A PHILOSOPHICAL DIGRESSION.

things we enjoy have been evolved, for this artificial development consists in combining in numberless different ways the natural material, and is the stage of evolution through which we are passing now.

"This boat which carries us so smoothly and swiftly, the houses we live in, the clothes we wear, the books we read, are simply combinations called into existence by the desire of men for pleasant sensations, or in other words, by their efforts to increase their happiness.

"I will not weary you by enlarging on this theme, but I will point out to you that it is of the utmost importance for our success that we should know if we are working in harmony with the forces which have brought the earth to the present stage of development. Whether we believe that progress is controlled by laws alone, or that it is directed by an intelligent power, the first condition of success is that we should work in harmony with the law of progress.

"But how shall we know that we are in accord with the march of civilization? Who shall decide when doctors disagree? We answer that if we can find what is the incentive to right conduct, we can tell by the result upon our happiness if our actions are in harmony with the advance of civilization. According to the law of progress as I have stated it to you, pleasant sensations are the motive power of civilization, and thus we believe that whenever our conduct causes an increase of pleasant sensations, it co-ordinates with the advance of civilization, which is equal to saying that the increase of happiness is the true standard of conduct.

"And it is thereon, Mr. Balcom, that our philosophy differs from that of all other civilized nations. They have moral codes, revealed laws, ancient maxims, but they have no standard of conduct by which they can test the correctness of their actions. We also have codes, laws, and maxims, but they are all derived from a scientific standard which provides a correct test for all our actions. This applies to the Commonwealth as well as to the individual. By that standard we test our public institutions, and find that those which secure the most happiness are also the most conducive to a high state of civilization, and by that standard each individual is taught to test his own actions, and soon learns by experience that the conduct which creates the most pleasant relations with his surroundings, is that which harmonizes the best with nature's laws and fosters his truest happiness.

"I do not know if this brief explanation will convince you. An entirely different philosophy has held the minds of Christian nations so long that it is difficult to weigh impartially the proofs of what we advance. For two thousand years the fear of Hell has brooded as a dark pall over the Christian world, and the whole study of conduct has been turned in the direction of learning how to serve the Lord and obey his commandments so as to escape the wrath to come. Success has been branded as the badge of wickedness, and enjoyments shunned as the temptations of our fallen and sinful nature. But the time has come when better knowledge has dissipated our fears, and an honest study of the subject has taught us that success in the realm of conduct means precisely the same that it means in the realm of other pursuits. It simply proves that we are acting in harmony with nature's laws, and we have as much right to all the happiness we can attain, as we have to the wages of labor faithfully performed. Pleasant sensations may be called the wages given by nature for conduct which it approves, and the larger the wages we receive, the more assurance we have that we are moving in the right direction.

"But whether I have convinced you or not, I have said enough to give you an outline of our philosophy. If it strikes

A PHILOSOPHICAL DIGRESSION. 23

you favorably, you can study it at leisure, and follow it in its numerous ramifications. It will bear the test of investigation, I assure you, and if once you accept it for your own, you will never regret it.

"And now let us pass to the practical objections to its adoption by the Commonwealth, which you presented to me this morning. How, do you ask, is the innate selfishness of men to be restrained? Who shall decide in case of a conflict of interests?

"Before answering you, I might put some questions myself. What leads you to believe that men are so selfish? Is it not because you have heard so much about their innate depravity that you fail to recognize the good there is in them? Are you sure the display of selfishness is not the result of the social conditions in which they have lived till now, and that competition is not largely responsible for it? Or have you ever experimented whether in a true Commonwealth there is so much antagonism between public and private interests?

"We have more faith than you in human nature, and are not afraid of a certain amount of selfishness, for we know that it underlays all attempts at improvement. But it must be tempered by sympathy. They are the centripetal and centrifugal forces of society, which ought to balance each other, and would do so if properly controlled.

"But your system of society fails to recognize the true functions of these forces, and selfishness has the control of the government, and no power is given to sympathy to restrain it. Selfish individuals are allowed to grasp all the valuable privileges, while sympathetic persons waste their efforts in vain attempts to palliate the sufferings endured by those who are worsted in the battle of life.

"We recognize the value of both factors, and instead of preaching against selfishness on one hand, and allowing it to run riot on the other, we keep it within proper limits by public measures, demanded and supported by the united sympathies of the community.

"The same sympathetic feeling prevents the Commonwealth from passing laws that would antagonize with the welfare of individuals, and leads it to encourage all its members who honestly try to improve their condition. But it is also the business of the Commonwealth to restrain those persons who would abuse their power to the detriment of others. The Commonwealth meddles as little as possible with private actions, but if any person presumes on its toleration to impose upon others, it promptly interferes and puts a stop to it. We try to be as a large family with many interests in common, and where there is a sympathetic bond uniting all its members, but if one of the family so conducts himself as to be unpleasant to others, the head of the family asserts his authority and obliges him to keep his proper place. The Commonwealth as a whole represents the head of the family, promoting the happiness of all its members, instructing and helping, with kindness towards all, but prompt to control when the public good requires it."

This, my dear Harry, is in substance what Mr. Walter told me, and I must acknowledge that it impressed me very favorably. Among the many points in its favor which presented themselves to me, I will only mention to you two which seem worthy of special consideration.

If he is correct, then society is slowly progressing towards a state of perfect harmony, where all factors will find their proper sphere and the highest civilization be attained, and we can explain the conflicts through which society passes now, and has passed up to this time, as the educative stage of mankind, and necessary to its full development. It is the social phase of the struggle for existence, and will eventually

A PHILOSOPHICAL DIGRESSION.

result in the survival of the most satisfactory public and private institutions.

The other point goes to confirm the claim made by Mr. Walter for the beneficent influence of the pursuit of happiness. His assertions brought to my mind some facts that have come under my notice. You know that I am interested in farming. Now I have often had occasion to see the influence of a correct standard upon the character and the social relations.

You recollect Mr. Daval, our neighbor. He has a high standard of farming, and is successful in his operations. He is not soft-hearted, but all the same his men are comfortably housed and are well and punctually paid; his horses are of the best and receive all the care they need, and his stock is well fed and sheltered. His relations with his men are always pleasant; he treats them well, and they know it and are anxious to remain in his service.

Not far from him lives Mr. Thornwald, a much kinder man and easy-going in all his business relations. But he is a poor farmer and everything about him is in a dilapidated state. His children leave him as soon as they can make their way in the world, his men are ill paid and dissatisfied, his horses are poor and his cattle half starved. All the difference in results comes from difference in aims. To accomplish his ends, Mr. Daval had to treat his surroundings right, even his fields which receive the best of care, and give him large returns.

Call it selfishness, or call it by any other name, the result has been to create around him a little community where exist the best conditions for men and beasts, while life in Mr. Thornwald's home is barely supportable.

These facts seem to me to point to an harmony in nature which compels us, if we would be happy, to help improve the conditions of our surroundings, which would go to prove that Mr. Walter's claims rest on a solid foundation.

CHAPTER V.

THE CHANGES MADE.

The morning was nearly spent before we had exhausted the subject, and yet nothing had been said about the social changes they had made in Socioland, although that was to be the topic of our conversation, and we were called to dinner before I could get Mr. Walter to tell me what they had done. At the table the conversation became general, and when we left it, some time elapsed before I could get him disentangled from his surroundings, and seated in a place where I felt safe from interruption.

"Now," said I, sitting down comfortably by his side, "you have treated me to a bit of history, and to an essay upon philosophy, let us come down to Socioland, and to what you have done to ameliorate its social conditions."

"Certainly, I will tell you with pleasure," he answered. "I see I have yet time enough before we reach Spencer. And for a beginning I will tell you of one of our first measures, which I believe would find favor in all countries and with all classes of people. We have abolished all taxes."

"What!" I exclaimed, "abolished all taxes! That is indeed a practical step towards happiness. But how then does your government raise the money to meet its necessary expenses?"

"Well," rejoined Mr. Walter, "it honestly earns it as every government ought to do. Our Commonwealth carries on business, earns money by legitimate means, and spends it for the benefit of all.

"The system of taxation, Mr. Balcom, firmly entrenched as it is in the habits of civilized society, is in fact a relic of barbarism. It is a remnant of the times when the strong lived altogether on the labor of the weak. Civilization has modified it, and the iron hand is more cunningly masked by the velvet glove, but the fact remains that the producer is made to support all the public burdens. Of course the Commonwealth must have means to defray the public expenses, but by what logical argument can it be maintained that if it is trusted to spend money, it cannot also be trusted to earn it? The truth is that when the ruling classes were compelled to surrender a portion of their privileges, and give the people a voice in the control of the government, they threw on the public all that which cost money, and under various pretexts kept in their own hands all the profitable enterprises. As plundering the producers was then the only known process for providing funds to carry on the government, it was legalized and made legitimate by acts of the legislatures, and legal taxation was organized. When that proved insufficient, and the people refused to bear heavier taxation, the rich, instead of giving of their surplus to supply the deficiency, lent to the government the money they had accumulated, and thus created for their own benefit a perpetual lien on the production of the country. To you, who are used to that system, it probably seems perfectly right and proper, but to us who have a much better way to provide for public needs, we look upon taxation as an unjust and needless imposition.

"But the release from taxation is not the only advantage which has resulted to the country from the management of business enterprises by the Commonwealth.

"We spoke yesterday of the growing evil of large fortunes. Our system has cut off the evil at its roots. Excessive fortunes are not the result of individual economy or persistent labor; they are the result of the cumulative power of capital. If you inquire into the origin of the vast fortunes which exist in your country, you will find that most of them are due to the investments of profits made in certain lines of business, carried for the benefit of the community. We readily acknowledge the need of those services, we know that under your system they could not be performed unless some persons had saved, often by great denial, the needed capital; nor do we believe that those services are over-paid. But we claim that the field of activity they opened was so vast that it enabled those persons to accumulate such large fortunes as to endanger the welfare of the community.

"Those are the lines of business we decided to withdraw from the field of competition, and to place in the hands of the Commonwealth, to be prosecuted for the benefit of all.

"That is the first change we have made in our internal economy. Our Commonwealth, instead of levying taxes from its citizens, carries on all the most extensive and profitable enterprises of the country, with the avowed object of making money to be spent for the good of the whole people.

"Thus, Mr. Balcom, we have accomplished what I told you was our aim. *We tap the Source of Excessive Wealth, and turn it into a Reservoir for the benefit of all classes.*"

Mr. Walter's information was interesting, for the changes he was describing seemed practical and well worthy of consideration. So I asked him to tell me which were the lines of business the Commonwealth had kept in its own hands, and how they were managed to avoid peculation and waste.

"My young friend," he answered, "the question of the management of public affairs is too large for us to go into now and you will be able to study it carefully while you stay in Socioland. But as to the lines of business we place in the care of the Commonwealth, I can state in broad terms that it is those which require large capital, and return through the magnitude of their operations large profits. For the present the Commonwealth controls the Wholesale Trade, the Trans-

THE CHANGES MADE.

portation of Letters, Parcels, Merchandise, and Persons, the Telegraph and Telephone, the Banks, the Life and Fire Insurances, the Street Railways, the Supply of Lights and Water, the Working of the Mines and a portion of the Manufactures.

"These, as you will see, are distributed between the Commonwealth and the several Townships, so as to take advantage of the best localities, and to secure the most efficient management. Each case is decided on its own merits, with due regard to the comfort and happiness of our whole people. We try to prevent the waste of competition, and the evils of undue personal accumulation of wealth, and to make our Commonwealth rich and prosperous so that it can reduce the expenses of living, increase the comfort of all its citizens, and protect the poor and disinherited against want and suffering.

"But let us pass on to other changes we have made. Let me tell you about our laws in regard to land."

I signified my desire to hear whatever he thought would interest me, and Mr. Walter continued.

"Our Commonwealth never admitted the right of individual ownership in land, and holds it in trust for the whole people. For purposes of improvement it sells leases, equal for practical purposes to complete ownership. These leases can only be cancelled if the public good requires it, and the tenant must be paid for actual damages inflicted upon him. No rent is paid, and those leases can be divided, bought and sold, but a limit has been placed upon the number of acres that each person can get under his control. By this policy, the Commonwealth has retained in its possession all the best business locations, or can reclaim them at reasonable rates. No property can be held for speculation, nor can any man or set of men levy exorbitant tolls in the shape of rents because they are the lucky owners of a piece of land so situated as to be indispensable to the efficient transaction of business.

"We hold that the land is common property, but we recognize also that its division among the people leads to a higher development and to better culture. We appreciate upon character the good effects of personal enterprise and independent management, provided they are kept within proper limits. It is only when private enterprise overshadows and antagonizes public welfare that we see to circumscribe it. This land policy of ours has been a success so far. It has stopped speculation in land, it has prevented the premature settlement of distant portions of our territory, and yet those of us who wanted to make a living by agriculture have been able to get possession of all they could cultivate."

"I think I understand the trend of your public policy," I remarked, when Mr. Walter ceased speaking. "You use the power of the Commonwealth to regulate the distribution of wealth. In the United States, we expect the government to insure political equality, while you add to the functions of yours the task of maintaining social equality. With this object in view, the means you use must exert a very good influence in that direction."

"Indeed you are correct, my dear Sir, and to insure the success of our scheme, we have made some radical changes in the methods of educating our young people.

"We claim that equal advantages in education are necessary to maintain equal chances of success in society. Furthermore we claim that it is of the utmost importance to educate and train the physical as well as the mental faculties.

"The education of the mind, the training of the intellect, can of course best be accomplished in the schools, and except that we have reduced the number of hours of study, and pay more attention to recreation, there is but little difference between our schools and yours. The great difference is in the industrial training of the youths of both sexes. The numerous

THE CHANGES MADE. 31

business enterprises carried on by the Commonwealth and the Townships offer splendid opportunities for practical training, and all our young people are compelled to serve a six years' term of apprenticeship to the state."

"It seems to me," I rejoined, "that it is a very arbitrary measure, and one that must create a great deal of dissatisfaction."

"It seems so to you," answered Mr. Walter, "because you are thinking of its application under the old conditions, but the public apprentice system is very popular with us. You will stay long enough among us to see how our youths are treated and understand why it is popular with them, and I can tell you why it is popular with the grown people also.

"By entrusting to our youths a large portion of the work connected with the business of the Commonwealth, we have opened to them an extensive industrial school, where there is an almost unlimited choice of occupations, and by requiring of them only a few hours of actual work, we give them ample time and facilities to keep on with their studies. Our system is far superior to your industrial schools, for our boys do not play with tools among other boys, but do real work alongside of men, under conditions which train the mind to face all kinds of emergencies, and compel them to exercise all the faculties they may possess. One year in an industrial school may teach a boy how to saw to a mark or plane a board straight, and may teach him many of the technicalities of his profession, but one year of apprenticeship will teach him all that and much more.

"So we believe in our apprentice system because it gives our youths the best training under the best possible conditions; we believe in it because it considerably reduces public expenses, and thus increases public wealth; we believe in it because it has had a moral result which has been satisfactory beyond our expectations.

"There is always a tendency among the children of the men who are the most successful, to believe that idleness and luxury are badges of superiority, and that they are made of different and better clay than those persons who are raised in the lower walks of life. Six years of apprenticeship, subject to uniform rules, and where merit is the only factor in promotion, generally takes such ideas out of their heads.

"Those, Mr. Balcom, are the changes we have made in the public policy of Socioland, and I have no doubt that when you see the results, you will acknowledge that we have succeeded, and that our people have much better facilities for the pursuit of happiness than can be found anywhere else.

"By making our Commonwealth a co-operative business concern, we have made it rich and placed all its citizens above want. We have entirely abolished overgrown fortunes and greatly diminished the accumulation of capital in private hands, and yet we have retained sufficient fields of activity for private enterprises, which being relieved from the pressure of monopolistic competition, give to their operators agreeable occupation and full reward for their labor.

"By retaining in the hands of the Commonwealth the control of the land, we have prevented its unjust distribution and sinful waste, and yet we have secured to all our citizens a fair chance to its acquisition.

"By our system of public apprenticeship we are training our youths to useful occupations, developing their bodies as well as their minds, and giving them a just appreciation of the conditions of life. It brings all classes together and equalizes their chances, and is without doubt the measure that will have the most far-reaching effects."

We were nearing Spencer, and I thanked Mr. Walter for his kindness to me, and the interest he had manifested in my desire to investigate.

"You are welcome indeed," he rejoined. "It is a pleasure to give information where it is so thoroughly appreciated. But we are nearly at the landing, and as I live in Spencer I hope to see you again and have more conversation with you, and that you will soon learn to know us and like us.

"Where do you intend to stay while in the city? You do not know. Well, I would advise you to stop at one of the hotels kept by the city, near the wharves and depots, for the convenience of travellers. You will be comfortable and the charges are very moderate. It will be more interesting than if you stop at a private boarding house in the center of the city, for it will be your first introduction to one of our public institutions."

CHAPTER VI.

AT THE HOTEL.

Spencer is the commercial center of Socioland, and is situated at the lower end of lake Norlay. It is the gateway of communication with the civilized world. Now a city of 50,000 inhabitants, it has a great future before it, and the characteristic American thought came to my mind of the fine field it would offer for speculation, were it not prevented by the land policy of the country.

We steamed slowly into port, and when we landed at the wharf, I looked around for some one to take me to the hotel. Mr. Walter was busy, yet found the time to poind out an official whose functions, he said, were to give information to travellers, and help them on their way. This gentleman, for undoubtedly he was one in appearance and demeanor, asked me where I wanted to go, and advised me to stop at the nearest City hotel, which was only a stone's throw from the landing. He also pointed to me the government baggage agent, a bright young man in uniform, who took the number of my check and the address to which I wanted my trunk sent, and after he had checked off on my baggage card the amount due for city transportation, I was ready to go on my way.

And here I may as well explain to you that in Socioland there are no ticket offices at the railroad depots or steamboat landings. Travelling cards are bought in the stores, good for a given number of miles. These cards are good on all roads or boats, in all directions and at all times. The conductor checks off the number of miles travelled, and when the card is used, a new one is bought. There are no excursion or return tickets, and the card does not give free transportation of baggage. Baggage cards are bought in the same way, good for transportation on the cars or boats, and also for transfer from the residences to the depots. The price of all these cards is exceedingly low, according to our standard, but with the exceptional facilities possessed by the Commonwealth, and the concentration of all the business in its hands, it is claimed the profit is quite rge. The freight business is also managed differently from ours. All goods must be prepaid, stamps being used for that purpose. These changes do away with some of the complications which increase the expenses in our country, but are only possible where all the means of transportation are concentrated in one hand.

I find, my dear Harry, that I am not making much progress in my journey, but I must manage to take you as far as the hotel, which proved to be a large brick building of plain appearance, with City Hotel No. 3, written on the facade and over the entrance. Its interior did not differ materially

AT THE HOTEL.

from our large hotels; probably as much comfort, but less luxury.

At the clerk's desk stood a bright young woman, who after I registered, had me shown to a room where I proceeded to make myself at home.

That which struck me at once, as we made our way to the upper regions where my room was located, was the number of young people who seemed to be busy in the house, and whom I concluded were some of the apprentices Mr. Walter had told me of. Both boys and girls wore plain uniforms, and were evidently engaged in doing the regular housework.

The afternoon was well advanced when we reached Spencer, and supper was ready by the time I had attended to my toilet. At the table, where a goodly number of guests were seated, we were waited on by these youths who performed their task with due courtesy, but without servility. The service was under the supervision of an elderly lady, who showed the guests to their places, and saw that their wants were provided for.

After supper, I strolled a while in the city, and when I returned to the hotel, made my way to the parlor, where I found, besides many of the guests, quite a number of young people in uniform, evidently the attendants of the house. These youths were not busy at work, but were engaged in social pastimes, and were treated on terms of social equality.

At the piano, a middle-aged gentleman and a pretty brunette were singing, while I recognized in the girl who played the accompaniment, one of our waiters at the table. The young man who had showed me to my room was one of a party who were playing cards, while many groups engaged in conversation were scattered in the room. Some of the ladies had their work, and there seemed to be very little formality, but plenty of mirth and good nature.

I quietly took a chair and watched the novel scene, wondering what our United States friends would say if the menials of an American hotel should invade the parlor and make themselves at home therein. But I soon reflected that these youths were not menials, as we understand the term, but that they were simply passing a term of apprenticeship which would fit them for the different duties of life, and that there was nothing more degrading in their work than there is in waiting upon customers in a store, or in working in a millinery establishment.

As I sat there, looking and thinking, a lady entered the room, and probably recognizing me as a stranger, and noticing my lonely position, came towards me and opened the conversation by a casual remark about the singers at the piano. As my principal object here is to get all the information I can, I managed to turn the conversation towards their peculiar method of treating the employees of the house, and remarked that I was a stranger in the land, and not used to their ways.

"Yes," said the lady, "it must be somewhat unexpected to find the help of the establishment enjoying themselves in the parlor, and must be a shock to your ideas of social position."

"It is indeed unexpected," I answered, "and at first it may have seemed undesirable, but I can see that these young people are sufficiently educated to be at home everywhere. No, what surprises me is, that they should be spared from their occupations, and I wonder how the work can be attended to and these boys and girls enjoy themselves at the same time."

"I understand that very well," she replied, "for our ways are in some respects so different from yours, that many things you will see here must naturally surprise you. We are able to give our youths plenty of time for recreation on account of the difference in our social system.

"In your country, a portion of the population has managed to throw the burden of labor on others, so that those on whom the burden has fallen have very little leisure time.

AT THE HOTEL.

With us it is entirely different. All our young people must do their share of work, and it is difficult for the adult to live in idleness here.

"Do you see that young girl," turning and pointing toward another part of the room, "talking to that bright-faced boy? She is the daughter of one of our best men in the town, a sensible, practical, business girl, with the same qualities which have made her father a successful man among us. With his business abilities, he would in your country have accumulated great wealth, and his daughter would have been educated to fill a leading place in society. The result would have been that she need never have done any work, and until she married would have led a useless life, supported by the exertions of the laboring poor. Besides the waste of her own time, she would have required the services of a waiting maid to attend to her artificial wants. Nor would she have been happier, for she is born for better things.

"Her life here has been entirely different. Her father has used his abilities for the benefit of the Commonwealth; as one of our Managers he has earned the trust and confidence of all who know him, and is in easy circumstances and no more. His daughter has had to do her share of the public work ever since she was fourteen, and thus has relieved of its extra burden some of her less fortunate sisters. As she learned the work, and her good qualities showed themselves, she has steadily advanced, and now fills a position of trust in this house.

"Thus you see that as we all have to do our share, none have to work very long or very hard, and we can give our young people time to rest, or study, or enjoy themselves, as they prefer. We use as little compulsion as possible in Socioland, but we provide ample facilities for study, and are anxious to encourage all that tends to the intellectual development of our children.

"You seem to be quite a believer in the public apprentice system," I remarked. "It is pleasant to find that the people here are satisfied with their institutions. A contented people is something very unusual nowadays."

"And it ought to be," the lady rejoined, "for all other nations are cramped by institutions they have outgrown, and no longer fit the intellectual stature they have reached. Here we are always ready to change whenever we have cause for dissatisfaction.

"But so far as our apprentice system is concerned, it is undoubtedly a great success. It greatly facilitates public business, provides pleasant employment for the young, and best of all, has proved a great educator, by teaching those who would be idle how to work, and by elevating the lower classes and educating them to hold their places among people of taste and culture.

"The girl I pointed out to you is an example of the first now if you will look in the direction of this window, I will show you an example of the other. That young man you see reading there is an orphan. His father, a common laborer, died young, leaving his family destitute. He came here from the old country and was a worthy man, but with little education. Under these conditions, in your country this boy would have had to go to work to help his mother, and would have remained an uneducated drudge all his life. With us, his mother was provided with a good place in one of the Town Laundries, where she receives liberal wages for short hours of labor, and thus was enabled to easily raise her family, while our apprentice system has given her boy an equal chance in the world with more favored children. He has been with us two years, and it has made a wonderful difference in him; his manner has greatly improved and he is getting interested in intellectual recreations.

AT THE HOTEL.

"But you see he has had opportunities which our system alone could give him, for it has brought him in close contact with much better educated persons than he was in the habit of associating with.

"The actual results of our system have been a steady gain in deportment and intelligence, and you will find no better behaved people than the inhabitants of Socioland, which is due to the training they receive in their youth.

"But have we not talked long enough on serious subjects, and would you not like to join us in some of the recreations of the evening? We have very pleasant times, I assure you, and it is largely due to the presence of our young people, for they make the charm of our social gatherings. Our travellers come and our travellers go, but our boys and girls are here all the time, ready to amuse and be amused. By freely mixing together we learn to know all about them. They tell us about their early lives, they confide to us their plans, their hopes, their dreams, and we give them the benefit of our experience, and try to make their life pleasant.

"But come, let me introduce you to Miss Bell, the lady I pointed out to you. You will enjoy her society, I believe, and when you get acquainted here, you will find that the time passes quite pleasantly."

I was easily persuaded, and was soon engaged in conversation, then joined in some games, and when I retired for the night, I thoroughly appreciated the friendly spirit which had so quickly made me feel at home among my new surroundings.

CHAPTER VII.

PUBLIC MANAGEMENT.

The lady with whom I had the conversation I reported to you, proved to be Mrs. Wilton, wife of the Manager of the hotel. I made the acquaintance of Mr. Wilton the next day, and had some interesting talks with him upon their methods of managing public business.

Mr. Wilton is an American, while his wife is a native of Socioland. He is about fifty years of age, and came here about fifteen years ago, having been in business in Cincinnati before he came to Spencer.

"Mr. Balcom," said he, "I understand that you should be surprised at our ways, for they are quite different from those of the United States. I was surprised myself when I first came, and wondered how business could be done in such easy-going ways. For we all take life easy here, and no one has to hurry out early in the morning or work till late at night. But understand me, I am speaking of productive labor. Of course we do not idle away such a large portion of our time, but we spend it in what we might call recreation, in so far that we all are at liberty to follow the dictates of our own sweet will, and use our time as we like best. But there is method in our madness, and if we have short hours of labor, we make good use of them, and if none work very hard or very long, all have to follow some useful occupation part of their time.

"Do you know that one of the most striking results of the policy of this people—of our policy, I might say, for I am entirely one of them—has been to so reduce the supply of labor for domestic services, that there are many things which it is much easier to do for ourselves than to hire done, and there are very few persons here who are not obliged to wait on themselves more or less. You see, when our young people have finished their term of apprenticeship, they all have a complete knowledge of some lucrative trade, and but few are found willing to do menial labor. This fact, added to the difficulty, if not the impossibility, of accumulating large fortunes, prevents the formation of a class who can command the services of others, and thus withdraws them from the field of production. Having no drones to support, we can accomplish much more, and still be able to considerably reduce the number of hours of labor.

"But excuse me, this was not the subject we were to talk about. You wished me to explain to you the way in which we manage public business."

"Yes, it is precisely what I want to know," I answered. "With us the assertion is usually made, with more or less truth, that whatever the government undertakes costs more than what is done by private management, and that the assumption of business by the state opens the door wide to mismanagement and corruption."

"Well, my dear Sir," Mr. Wilton replied, "I have not been here so long but what I can recollect how things went in the United States, and probably there is a foundation for the opinion you now express, although it may be fostered by those who have a direct interest in preventing the government from extending its operations.

"But there is a fundamental difference between your government and ours. Yours is a Republic, established to maintain civil and political rights. Ours is a Commonwealth, organized to secure those rights, and besides, to manage public business for public benefit.

"The founders of your Republic had no idea of national

co-operation for business purposes, for post offices, railroads, street-cars, the lighting of streets, etc., was then unknown, and when your Republic tries to manage business enterprises, it tries to accomplish something for which it has never been organized.

"A republican government is in theory a part of the people, but in practice is something above it. You elect your representatives to make your laws, and your officers to execute them, and so long as they hold their mandates, they are your masters as much as if they had been appointed by a king.

"There is no inducement to abuse that power so far as civil rights are concerned, but it is only a question of time for the men you elect to find out that a representative government can grant, against the will of the people, lucrative places, and legislate men into valuable positions where they can be taken care of out of the proceeds of taxation. All financial places of trust are in the gift of political officers, and are disposed of as rewards for personal services. Men thus appointed cannot be expected to be competent or trustworthy, and all kinds of safeguards have to be thrown around them to keep them in the path of honesty.

"Yours is the Individualistic system, where the whole aim of the government is to help the individuals to develop the resources of the country by affording equal protection to all its citizens.

"But a stream never rises higher than its source. A nation where the individual is taught to look upon himself as entered upon a race for wealth, where the winner reaches the goal exhausted by the efforts he has made to distance his competitors, where individual greed is encouraged by the most tempting rewards, and where a most intricate system of laws, courts and prisons, is needed to preserve some kind of order among the contestants will never evolve the right kind

PUBLIC MANAGEMENT.   43

of a government, or organize a satisfactory public management.

"It is something to have succeeded in restraining competition within legal bounds, but you will have to entirely change your policy before you can inaugurate the true Commonwealth, and when you try to apply the machinery of your representative government, to the management of business interests, you fail of entire success because it gives too much power to your public officers and legislatures.

"Our Commonwealth is organized in a different spirit and with a different purpose. It not only aims to preserve peace and order, but also to co-ordinate our producing power, and to make all its citizens participate in the increased production. Thus our welfare is intimately connected with the pecuniary success of the Commonwealth, and we are all interested in its proper management. On that account the people never surrender the law-making power to their delegates, but exercize a constant supervision over all their actions, and if they fail to properly conduct the business committed to their care, they are quickly called to account for their mismanagement."

"You do not then," I said, "surrender to your political officers the business interests of the country, and do not expect your President and Governors to manage them through agents of their own selection."

"No, not at all. In the first place we have no Presidents or Governors, their functions being filled by the Chairmen of the executive committees, but if we had, we would not place our financial interests in their hands.

"We have added to our government a Business department, independent of the Political and the Judiciary, which has entire charge of the business enterprises of the Commonwealth, and is responsible to the people alone for the result of their labor. Through this department we co-ordinate the producive power of the whole people, and constitute ourselves into a co-operative association. It creates a bond through the community of interests, and tends to destroy the spirit of competition among us.

"We, the people, thus become a business firm, and hire a certain number of men to manage the work for us. We recognize that if those men are competent, they are much better situated than we can be to know what is the best course to follow to succeed, and we place in their hands both power and responsibility. We recognize also that there must be stability, and on that account the Managers and Advisers are elected for indefinite terms, and are retained in place so long as the people are satisfied with their services. But should dissatisfaction arise, specific charges must be laid before the Advisers for investigation, and if they are sustained, a new election is ordered, which is the final verdict pronounced by the people. Thus we are learning the art of self-government, and while liable to make mistakes, they are corrected as soon as discovered.

"Those, you see, are the principles that govern us in the organization of the Business department. Elections of officers by the people, responsibility to the people, confidence in them so long as they give satisfaction, recall of their powers by the people whenever they are no longer pleased with their management."

"These principles," I remarked, "seem sound enough in theory, but may work badly in practice. The people who control your machinery are often a very unwieldy element. 'What is everybody's business is often nobody's business,' is a saying which contains more truth than poetry, and I should be afraid that the public supervision of which you speak would prove inefficient and easily evaded."

"You are right," answered Mr. Wilton, "and it is partly on that account that we have established Advisory Boards.

"The functions of these Boards are three-fold. To advise, to

PUBLIC MANAGEMENT.

supervise, to co-ordinate. They are clothed with no authority except such as they need to enable them to attain the needed information, and report to the people through publication.

"It is to them that we look for that close supervision so necessary to success. Their duties are to overlook the whole business situation, reconcile the different interests, keep watch over the receipts and the expenses, study the best means to promote the general welfare, and suggest them to the public and to the Managers.

"They are the oil which lubricates the co-operative machine. Their position enables them to take a broad look at the situation, and to give impartial information. As they occupy places of great influence, we are careful to select men of good judgment and known integrity, for our material prosperity depends largely upon the soundness of their advice.

"But as I have named the Managers, let me explain to you what are their functions. Their name is the best explanation I can give you, for they really manage the business placed in their charge, and within their departments have full authority placed in their hands. I am the Manager of this hotel, and have all the needed power to run it successfully, provided I use that power according to the recognized policy of the Commonwealth. Our position is somewhat like that of the captain of a vessel. A ruler on board, a private citizen on shore.

"Some of our Managers are elected by the Commonwealth, for they direct enterprises which must be under a central control, but all local business is controlled by Managers elected by the Townships, a division we have adopted in place of counties or incorporated cities, and which replaces them both. These Townships have each a business department of their own which looks after their local interests.

"We have, as I told you, formed ourselves into a business firm, and have tried to follow the same course that a practical business man would take under the same circumstances.

"Success demands a general direction by men who can overlook the whole field of operations, and co-ordinate to a successful end the means under command. We secure this through our boards of Advisers, whose duty it is to gather information, and furnish it to the inhabitants of the Commonwealth. We do not entrust them with the execution of the measures they recommend, because it would give them more power than any man, or set of men, should have except in times of public danger.

"The next thing that success demands is an efficient executive management, which shall not be hampered by intricate laws and regulations, but left free to attain the desired ends in the best manner consistent with the means placed at its disposition. This, we secure through our Managers, who, elected by the people, and responsible to the people alone, have every inducement to fulfil their task to the best of their ability.

"Next, we must have a division of responsibility, which we secure through our system of Townships, which are really branches of the whole firm or Commonwealth, having special interests under their control.

"Believing as we do that co-operation ought to replace competition as far as possible, that each individual has social as well as political rights, and that a Commonwealth which helps its citizens to attain to a fair share of comfort and enjoyment is as far superior to a Republic as a Republic is to Despotism, we have tried to secure that result through our organization.

"We have retained political and judicial organizations, but their importance is steadily diminishing, not because their functions are encroached upon by the business department, but from the results of our policy, which are constantly diminishing the causes which compel the enactment of laws and the need of restraint. All wars, disputes, contentions, are the outcome of the competitive spirit, either in nations or individuals, and whatever promotes the co-operative interests, diminishes the spirit of greed which has to be restrained by law, and thus diminishes the need of the laws themselves.

"We believe in social equality, in the solidarity of human interests, and instead of using our skill and intelligence in trying to remedy the evils of society by law, we use our intelligence in devising means to diminish the need of laws by creating harmonious relations between man and man."

Mr. Wilton then had to leave, so I thanked him for his information, hoping to hear more at some future day.

CHAPTER VIII.

THE RIGHT SPIRIT.

Several days passed before I renewed my conversation with Mr. Wilton, days which I spent in viewing the city and its surroundings, and also in getting acquainted with the people. Undoubtedly there is a difference between life here and in the United States; as much, I suppose, as there is between life in the United States and in Europe.

One thing is quite noticeable. It is that they know how to work and how to enjoy themselves. During working hours everything seems to move briskly, each one has something to do, and without any fuss and worry, an immense amount of work is accomplished. But the working hours are short, and when they are over, one might believe himself in one of those Italian cities, where after sunset it looks as if the whole population had turned out to enjoy an evening stroll in the open air.

The stores open late and close early, especially the wholesale stores which do not keep open more than six hours. The retail stores, which are left to private enterprise, keep open longer, but no one is found willing to work from early morning till late at night, as so many are obliged to do under our system. The more even distribution of wealth has fostered a quieter spirit, and as great accumulations of property are not possible, and poverty is practically unknown, there are none of those strong incentives to extra exertions which are found in other countries.

I have made some casual acquaintances in my rambles, and have had some conversations with persons I met on the cars or in the stores, and I find everywhere the same satisfaction with existing conditions.

In a retail store I entered to buy underwear, I found the owner to be a quiet, unassuming old gentleman, who liked to talk, and who told me some things that go to show the influence which surrounding conditions have in modifying character.

"I am surprised," I said to him, "at the easy way in which you do business here, and that some of your energetic men do not take advantage of it to crowd to the wall their less ambitious neighbors."

"I believe," he answered, "that if you were to remain here some time, you would understand it better. It is natural that in your country you should strive for wealth, for wealth is not only comfort. it is more, it is power.

"Under your system everything is for sale, and the man of wealth can get possession of everything which is worth having. Your rich men own your railways, your street cars, your steamboats. They own your palaces, your most valuable lands, the stores and the goods they contain. They own the manufactures, the banks and the money, and worse yet, they own mortgages upon the homes of the workers and upon their future production in the shape of public bonds.

"But it is not so here. Suppose I should bestir myself to accumulate a fortune, what should I do with it? All our most valuable property is in the hands of the Commonwealth and cannot be bought at any price. We have no government bonds or railroad stocks to furnish investments here. There is a small demand for private capital, mostly for manufacturing purposes, but on account of the high price of labor, and the abundance of money furnished by the Commonwealth, interest is very low, and we have little inducement to increase our wealth beyond what will secure us a comfortable existence."

With my ideas fresh from America, where wealth is all powerful and its acquisition the chief end in life, I expressed my astonishment that the people of Socioland should be satisfied under such a regime, and my fear that this stifling of private ambition might result unfavorably to the general prosperity.

"Yes, yes," said my new acquaintance, "you reason precisely as would have done, some hundred years ago, a French marquis or a German baron. They could not have understood that life was worth living in a country without an army and without an aristocracy. Yet you have learned in America that there are other things worth living for besides parading at Court or killing our fellow-men, and we have found out here that there are other things worth living for besides the acquisition of money.

"But you are entirely mistaken in your supposition that a diminution of private ambition will have a bad influence on the public prosperity.

"Our men have as much brain, as much physical activity,

and are just as enterprising as yours, and as ready to conceive and execute, but, unable to concoct schemes by which they can exploit their weaker neighbors for their own benefit, they have to place their intelligence and their activity at the disposal of the Commonwealth to be used for the people's benefit.

"My dear Sir," and the old gentleman getting a little excited, emphasized his words so as to bring the whole weight of his argument to bear upon me, "which do you suppose displayed the truest ambition. The freebooter baron of old who, at the head of a band of private retainers, plundered the unwary traveller for his personal advantage, or the officer of a modern army, fighting for the preservation of the whole country? Yours is the freebooter system, where 'Every one for himself and the Devil take the hindmost' is the motto inscribed on your banner, while ours is the organized army of labor, where individual effort is trained to promote the welfare of all.

"No, no, this old argument of the decline of enterprise under a better co-operative system will not stand fire or hold water. It is based upon a false estimate of human nature, and experience disproves it every day. Even in your country the greatest achievements have been done under government auspices, and the best work is done by men who have no financial interest in the result of their labor.

"You may have in your midst men who, under the incentive of private gain, will do more and be keener in the pursuit of wealth than they would be were they working for public benefit, but also how many men with as keen intellect they may crush, and how many efforts they may cause to abort in their struggles to distance their competitors! All of which is clear loss to the Commonwealth, and may more than balance the gain made by those who are successful.

THE RIGHT SPIRIT.   51

"Not only do we escape this waste of energy, but our efforts at improvement are better co-ordinated and better sustained, for they are backed by the whole power of the Commonwealth. The result is that we are a wealthy people, producing at less cost than other nations, and far beyond our daily wants."

I did not try to answer the old gentleman, for really I did not know what to say. My objections could not be founded on practical knowledge, but on preconceived ideas fostered by education. These people had tried their system and were satisfied. Still it seemed to me that all this government control could not be maintained without a serious loss of personal freedom.

I expressed my thoughts to my new acquaintance, and asked him whether, for instance, he was not compelled to order his goods from certain stores, and give for them a price arbitrarily fixed by the government?

"Not at all," he answered. "It is strange how the idea of compulsion clings to whatever is connected with government control. Our wholesale trade is perfectly free, and the prices are regulated by the law of supply and demand as in all other countries. It is in the hands of the Townships instead of being in private hands. That is all the difference. I order where I please and what I please and every one does the same. It is true that we have some regulations here that do not exist in other countries, but they are for the protection of the whole people. One is a regular scale of profits, without any admixture of speculation in it. I know that the price I give the Town for the goods bears a regular ratio to the price paid to the producer and manufacturer, and I also know that I have nothing to fear from those speculative fluctuations in price which so often ruin the most careful dealer.

"Another rule is that we must pay the cash. The Commonwealth furnishes an abundance of money for all transactions, and as it never speculates, we have no panic or stringency in the money market. We, the merchants, are not at the mercy of the bankers, and the whole trade of the country is never paralyzed because these money kings feel the need of protecting themselves.

"Again there is one wholesale price for all. The price of goods in all wholesale stores is open to inspection, and our customers can buy at the same price we do if they buy in sufficiently large quantities. We are only distributors whom the people are willing to pay for their trouble, but there is no chance for exorbitant profits.

"Thus by a few simple rules, which are approved of by all sensible persons, and from the power which results from their position, the Townships are able to regulate all the trade, to insure to the customers a large choice of goods at the minimum cost of distribution, and protect them against speculation.

"Outside of these regulations the most perfect freedom exists, and I can deal with another Township, or with the manufacturer direct if I find it to my advantage. Besides, many articles, as fruits, vegetables, meats, milk and others of a perishable nature, never find their way to the wholesale stores, but are left to private hands. We are not working out any definite plan, and would as soon leave the wholesale trade to private citizens if the result was more satisfactory. But our system enables us to better provide for the people, and to protect them from trusts and other speculative combinations. And the profits derived from the wholesale trade form one of the most available public revenues.

"As for the question of individual freedom, you are I think entirely mistaken. The well digested regulations, approved of by the majority of the people, and enforced by the Commonwealth, are not nearly as oppressive as the rules arbitrarily enacted according to the whims of the money kings. Order is one of the conditions of society, and must be enforced either by private edicts or public laws. All that we can ask is that they should be such as tend to accomplish the desired end with the least infringement of individual freedom. We willingly submit to the government's control, but we never would stand the treatment you receive from private corporations, who have no respect for the desires of their customers, except so far as it can influence the amount of money they expect to make out of them.

"Besides, we have extended the sphere of personal freedom, and are willing to leave private conduct to be regulated by natural results, and many laws which are yet in force among you, would not be tolerated an instant here."

Much more did the old gentleman tell me, for we talked a long time, and I must acknowledge that the more I understand the spirit which controls their public organization, the more I believe that they are moving in the right direction.

CHAPTER IX.

THE APPRENTICES.

The next day I had occasion to resume my conversation with Mr. Wilton. I am getting very much interested in all I see and hear, and while I do not find Socioland different in its features and products from other countries I have visited, I recognize that Mr. Walter was right when he warned me that I would find myself in an entirely different atmosphere. This does not appear on the surface, although indications can be seen by the careful observer, but its influence is strongly marked on their internal economy. I am more and more convinced that they are in a fair way of solving problems which have puzzled mankind for a long time, and I desire to learn all I can as to the manner in which they are solving them. So I was glad to find the next evening that Mr. Wilton had no previous engagement, and could spare the time for a long conversation.

After a few words on general subjects, I asked him to tell me more about the management of public business, especially of that part connected with the apprentices, for I meet them at every turn, and they are one of the most conspicuous features of the society in Socioland.

"I can probably best explain what you want to know," said Mr. Wilton in answer to my questions, "by giving you a short account of the management of this hotel. When the Township of Spencer, for reasons we will not go into now, decided to open another hotel, the first thing to be done was to select a suitable spot upon the land in its possession, and upon that tract to erect a building for that purpose. This was done by the Town Architect under the supervision of the Board of Advisers, the means coming from the surplus fund, which, with the resources in the hands of the Township, is always large.

"All the material was paid for in cash, that which came from the Township stores, as well as that bought from private persons. The labor was hired by the day or the week at liberal rates, but as many apprentices as possible were kept at work, to reduce expenses, and also because we find that physical exercise of that kind is a good training for our young men, and has a beneficial influence on their body and on their mind.

"And here, Mr. Balcom, let me point to you the difference between our system and that of the United States. In the building of this hotel we have eliminated the profit on the

THE APPRENTICES. 55

land which would have gone to some speculator, the profit on the material, which was mostly furnished by the wholesale stores, and the profit of the contractor. That which has cost us more money has been the labor which commands high prices here, yet the final result has been to reduce the cost one third. All this has been achieved without doing injustice to any one, but simply by preventing the monopolization of natural resources by individuals.

"When the house was finished, I presented myself as candidate for Manager. I have been connected with hotels all my life, and since my arrival in Socioland have been Head Steward in another establishment. I had borne a good character, and was elected without opposition. I have given satisfaction and have held the place ever since. My salary is liberal, but not extravagant, and I am well satisfied.

"As soon as elected, I took charge of the house which was not yet furnished. That part of the outfit was purchased under my care, conjointly with one of the Advisers who was detailed to help me until the work was finished. I furnished the knowledge of what would be required, while he safeguarded the interests of the Town. We were not limited in our expenses by an appropriation, but confidence was placed in our judgment and in our integrity.

"When the work was done, the full Board was invited to carefully examine the hotel throughout, the accounts were submitted to their inspection, and when all was recognized as correct, both the Architect and myself were notified that our work was satisfactory, and a notice to that effect, as well as a full statement of all our expenses, was published for the benefit of the inhabitants of Spencer.

"Once in charge, I proceeded to hire help, and besides, made an application to the Apprentice Bureau for as many of them as I thought I could employ. Those young people, who receive no wages, and are often very intelligent and anxious to learn, are a great help to reduce expenses, and there is always a great demand for them.

"When we put in a requisition, we must state the kind of occupation we have, for it is not only the apprentices just called out that are free to choose to work for us, but all those in the Commonwealth. Except that all apprentices are expected to keep at work, they have all the freedom of choice they can desire. At any time a young man or woman working for me can leave if they have a place offered to them where they think they would be better satisfied, but I can also send back to the Bureau any of them who does not give me satisfaction. Of course there are checks to the abuse of these privileges, for the Commonwealth has the welfare of its young people very much at heart, and the Apprentice Bureau is specially charged to see after them, and to advise them so as to prevent unwise changes. The parents have also influence with their children, and are consulted by the Bureau and the Managers so as to attain the best results.

"It is also the duty of the Bureau to investigate the complaints of the apprentices, and if, as sometimes happens with Managers newly elected, it is found that they cannot get along with the young people, it is considered a sufficient reason to put in motion the machinery necessary to secure a new election. We have also among our children some who have a roving disposition, and want to change often and without good cause. For these, places are found with Managers specially qualified to deal with such characters, and they are compelled to remain until there is an improvement in their disposition. Thus, without strict rules or harsh measures, we try by a process of natural selection to make the most of the material at our command.

"Once provided with a suitable building and the necessary

THE APPRENTICES. 57

personel, I am left free to run this hotel as if I owned it myself. I am expected to charge moderate prices, to give satisfaction to my guests, to deal kindly with my help, and to clear a moderate profit. I must keep a strict account of my receipts and expenses, which I can easily do with the help of the apprentices, several of whom are fair accountants and book-keepers. My accounts must always be open to the inspection of the Board of Advisers, or whoever they choose to delegate.

"The result of this union of responsibility and freedom is to create a body of men trained to the management of public enterprises, and we are educating the growing generation in the special qualifications needed for the responsible position of Managers. It is the process of the survival of the fittest applied to public affairs, and makes Socioland the best managed country in the world."

"But, Mr. Wilton," I remarked, "do you not have trouble with some of the apprentices? Of course the most of them are to be trusted, but are not several of them careless and unreliable, and more anxious to play than to work?"

"No," he answered. "We have very little trouble in that direction. Probably it is due to the spirit which reigns in Socioland and which affects all our people, and has its influence even upon the children. In the first place, all kinds of work are honorable here, and a moderate amount is looked upon as healthy for both body and mind. Our children are not taught that labor is a curse entailed upon the human family by the fall of Adam. On the contrary, they are taught that it is through labor that all that which makes life worth living has been attained, and that further progress will only result from labor intelligently directed. Then we teach them the great advantages which result from the combination of labor, and try to make them understand that concerted action is only possible when the right kind of spirit animates the whole population.

"As our aims are different from yours, we preach to our youths an entirely different doctrine. Your sins are the sins against the will of God, ours are the sins against the welfare of society. You trust in the authority of the law, we trust in each other, and frown down any conduct which tends to destroy this confidence. You envy and try to imitate the man who enriches himself at public expense; we look upon him as a public enemy. You excuse the man who betrays a public trust; we look upon him with the same contempt as the brave soldier looks upon the man who runs away in the midst of battle. We thus create a public spirit which is an important factor toward the success of our institutions.

"No, Mr. Balcom, we have very little trouble with our apprentices. Having a common aim and common interests, the desire for success permeates all our people and is felt by our children, so that they are willing to do their part, and those whose character inclines to neglect their work, are morally compelled to keep step with their surroundings.

"However there are other causes which induce our apprentices to work cheerfully. We try as far as possible to make them happy, and want them to enjoy life as much as the conditions permit. We believe in happiness, and want our children to be happy. They are not only well cared for, but as you have seen, they have much more recreation and also much more freedom than they have in your land. We ask nothing from them in the way of work but what they can see is for the general good, and when their task is accomplished, not only do we leave them free to do what they please, but we help them to spend their time agreeably and profitably."

"That, Mr. Wilton," I remarked, "must be a very good plan for boys and girls of good disposition, but we would be afraid

THE APPRENTICES.

to give so much freedom to our children, for it must be a great temptation to abuse the privilege, and form habits and associations which might have a bad influence on the character."

"You give me here, Mr. Balcom, a very old argument against every extension of individual freedom, an argument which is logical enough in the mouth of a Christian who believes in innate depravity, and is taught to pray to be kept out of temptation, but which, if you will allow me to say so, is entirely out of place in the mouth of an Agnostic and an American citizen.

"You, as an Agnostic, cannot believe in natural depravity, and as an American, you ought to know that the same criticism is launched at you by the Europeans on account of the greater freedom you give to the youths of both sexes, and yet you have no reason to believe but what their conduct is just as good as that of their European brothers and sisters.

"No, our experience has shown us that we can better afford to trust our young people than to mistrust them, and that if we taught them right we could safely allow them to control their own personal actions.

"Besides all these influences, our system is such as to induce our apprentices to their best exertions, for it is those who learn and improve, and show the most executive ability, who advance in position. There is really more incentive to well doing in our system than there is under private competition for the best prizes are won by actual merit, and not by favor or the privilege of birth.

"I have tried to explain to you, Mr. Balcom, how we try to foster from the start the spirit which alone can make our public policy a success. That is the base, the foundation, which lacking would wreck all our efforts. Public institutions are built upon private character, and the marked advance we think we have made over other nations, we would soon lose unless we cultivate the same spirit which animated our predecessors."

This opinion of Mr. Wilton is worthy of a careful study. If he is correct, then a change in public spirit must precede a change in public institutions. The lessons of history would show that he is right, for several times, under the leadership of progressive men, nations have tried to advance further than was warranted by the state of public knowledge, and after short trials the ground gained was lost, and the people had to fall back to their original institutions.

CHAPTER X.

ABOUT EDUCATION.

I am staying longer in Spencer than I had at first intended, but I am enjoying myself at the hotel, where I have many friends, and where reigns a home feeling which I had never found in a hotel before.

This feeling is not due to the special character of the guests, but is due to the social feeling among the employees of the hotel, young and old. As their tasks are comparatively light and they have much spare time, and as special efforts are made to spend this time in common, they constitute a social circle open at all times to the guests, and form the bond that keeps this pleasant home feeling alive. Every afternoon quite a number of people meet in the parlor, and every evening some entertainment is provided.

I find that music is very much cultivated in Socioland, and the children are taught to play and sing in the public schools.

ABOUT EDUCATION.

There are many good performers on several instruments among the hotel people, and concerts are of frequent occurrence. As for dancing, it is the order of the day here, and children are taught to dance almost as soon as they can walk. Besides these social advantages, there is a good library in the hotel, and it is well patronized.

On the other hand, there is very little style and it is not encouraged. Everything is nice and good, and all conveniences for comfort are provided for, but there is very little for show. The table is well supplied, and the service sufficient for those who are willing to eat at leisure.

One thing which makes it much easier for the people of the hotel and which is characteristic of the habits of the country, is that there is little or no travel at night.

In adjusting the time tables of public conveyances, the comfort of the employees is consulted as much as the desires of the travelling public, and they are so arranged as to prevent their being called upon to work at undue hours. That seemed very strange to me at first, for it is an unheard of thing among us that the convenience of the workers should be consulted in the running of public conveyances, and I could not understand that the travellers should be satisfied, but I learned that it is one of the natural consequences of the emancipation of the laborer from the thraldom of poverty.

In a country where a large part of the public labor is done by the young people, and where wealth is so distributed that want stares no one in the face, and where the attainment of happiness is made the chief incentive to labor, it would be unlogical to request the public employees to turn night into day for the convenience of those who want to be carried at night. Not that all night work can be dispensed with, only it is reduced to its minimum.

Such a course would be impossible with us for everything

is rushed through at railroad speed, and the motto "Time is money" is a true index of the practices of our country. But here if time is also money, yet money is not valued above comfort, and it will not buy the discomfort of a large portion of the people as it will do among us.

You may remember that the first day of my arrival I was presented to Miss Bell, whom Mrs. Wilton told me was the daughter of one of the influential men of Spencer, one of the class who among us would be a merchant prince and a financial power. I was very much pleased with her from that evening, and as she seems to enjoy my society, we have become very good friends indeed. She is not strikingly handsome, but is a pleasant looking girl of about nineteen years of age. She is a little above the medium height, with fair hair and honest blue eyes. One of those girls who improve in looks as they advance in years, and make the best of wives and mothers. I have not fallen in love with her, so my dear Harry, do not weave a little romance at my expense, but I find her well-informed and intelligent, and we enjoy conversing together. Miss Bell is as much interested in learning something of our usages as I am in learning from her, and it adds greatly to the pleasure of our conversation.

"Tell me, Mr. Balcom," she said to me one evening as we were sitting in the parlor, "how do girls of my age spend their time in the United States?"

"Ah! Miss Bell," I replied, "that is too hard a question for me to answer, for it depends very much in what station of life they are born."

"That is true," she remarked, "I had forgotten you told me that you have no public apprentices there. Do you know it seems impossible to realize that there should be so much difference in the education of children? Now here all have an equal chance, and the only difference is what results from our special ability, or from the choice of vocations. But tell me, how would I have been educated had I been born in the United States?"

"Well, Miss Bell, I will tell you as near as I can. You would have lived in a very large house, surrounded by a great many servants who would have waited on you, and would have been nearly all your society until you were old enough to go to school."

"What!" she exclaimed, "and my parents?"

"Oh! your father would have been too busy getting rich to spend much time at home, and too tired and nervous to stand the effervescence of your overflowing spirits, and as for your mother, the demands of society would have absorbed all her time, and she would have been compelled to leave you in the care of the nursery maid.

"You would have been first sent to private school, then to a finishing school until you were twenty years or more, when you would have come out in society, and spent your time in dressing, and making and receiving calls."

"Do you mean to say, Mr. Balcom, that I would have been kept at school more than ten years of my life? And what do these girls learn during all that time?"

"Really, Miss Bell, it is more than I can tell you. So far as I can judge, what they learn they keep to themselves, for I have never been able to detect it in their conversation. I have some times asked them what they learned at school and they would answer latin, algebra, geometry, chemistry, etc., but I never could get them to tell me what was the object of their studies, or how it was expected that it would help them through life."

"But surely, Mr. Balcom, these girls do not spend all their time in such studies. They must be taught some practical knowledge, something of housekeeping or cooking, or dressmaking.

something that will be of use to them in their married life."

"All that must seem strange to you, Miss Bell. It ought to be incredible, but it is a fact that in the United States the daughters of rich men are not expected to do any useful work in their life. What is expected of them is to adorn society, and they are taught accomplishments to enable them to fill in a graceful manner their appointed place. These accomplishments would be well enough if these girls had a useful background to hang them upon, but they know nothing of life and its realities, and have no desirable aims or serious purposes. They form among themselves a sort of mutual admiration society, where the false coin of fashion passes in place of the real currency of this busy world, and are failures so far as the welfare of mankind is concerned.

"Of course you understand that I am talking now of the daughters of our richest men, but unhappily they are the children of our most energetic and intelligent citizens, those best qualified to maintain a high standard of womanhood, and the number of girls so educated is increasing all the time. Their position makes them leaders in fashion, and all those persons who want to raise themselves in society follow in their footsteps, and actually believe that this useless education is a mark of distinction, and stamps its recipients as something superior to the rest of humanity.

"We think we have made a great advance because we have abolished the aristocracy of birth, but we have replaced it by an aristocracy of wealth, and the lessons of history are repeating themselves. Our aristocracy, instead of cultivating the qualities which have raised it above the common level, educate their children in idleness and uselessness, and thus fail to maintain the high standard they have attained, and demoralize all below them by the pernicious example of their luxurious lives."

"I cannot help believe, Mr. Balcom, that it is only one side

ABOUT EDUCATION.   65

of the picture you are showing me now. You must have a large number of girls who receive a practical and an intellectual education, and who, like us here, can turn their hands and brains to all kinds of useful occupations, possessing culture and accomplishments, and feeling at home everywhere."

"Of course we have," I answered. "The force of circumstances teaches many a girl the practical side of life, but it is not looked upon favorably, even by the most sensible portion of the community. The rich set the fashion, and all other classes follow as far as their means will allow. You have a check here on such pernicious influences in your social institutions which prevents the private accumulation of wealth, and trains all your people to useful occupations, but we have no checks, and the evil is running riot, and is fast demoralizing society.

"The results of our system of education are just as bad among the lower classes. Their children are not taught any useful knowledge, such as would help them to rise in the world, and our cities are full of girls who have to earn their living and are thrown upon their own resources without any preparation. You can have no idea, Miss Bell, of the misery of their existence. Ignorant, ill-paid, overworked, they are surrounded by their rich sisters, who flaunt in their faces their carriages and their silk dresses, and monopolize all the enjoyments.

"No, you cannot realize here how great a difference there is in the education of our children, and how far from an equal chance our system—or to be correct our lack of system—gives them of reaching a desirable position in society."

"But, Mr. Balcom, if it is as you represent it, why do you not adopt some system like ours?"

"You cannot understand," I answered, "how difficult it is to make changes in old settled countries. Many of us want a change, and in time will be sufficiently numerous to compel a change. The dissatisfaction with the inequalities in conditions is becoming greater every year, and it is one of the most encouraging signs of the times.

"It is only of late that this dissatisfaction has dared to manifest itself, for the religious beliefs of the past were opposed to changes, and their tendency was to encourage abject submission. For centuries the poor have been taught that God had created the existing conditions of society, and that he had chosen some to be rich and powerful, and others to be poor and submissive, and that any attempt to change these social relations was an act of rebellion against the decrees of an all-wise Providence.

"Those are, I suppose, arguments against progress you never heard before, and which would have no effect on you, and you would probably laugh at the person who told you that health or sickness, success or failure, happiness or misery, are not the result of the wisdom or foolishness of our actions, but the result of the will of God.

"Yet for ages this doctrine has been preached to us by those who were regarded as best qualified to teach, and any doubt as to its truth has been threatened with fearful punishment in a future existence. This doctrine is no longer believed, although it is still preached and listened to with respect, and the number of persons who believe that it is possible to equalize the social conditions is yet far too small to enable us to accomplish any important change.

"We are just emerging out of the toils of an iron-bound spiritual despotism, which has held society so long in its embrace that now that its arms are beginning to be loosened we are yet so cramped that very few realize that we are free to stretch out and seek for a more comfortable position. We commence to dare to express our belief that our position is not as satisfactory as it might be, and to deny the claims of those who oppose changes from fear that they might prove disastrous to their spiritual authority, but we are not yet far enough advanced as a people to know how to modify our public institutions.

"You can see, Miss Bell, by what I tell you, how much there is to be done before we can improve a state of society which is not only far from perfect, but fails utterly to promote the highest happiness of the rich as well as of the poor."

CHAPTER XI.

ANCIENT INSTITUTIONS.

I had not realized, my dear Harry, until I conversed with Miss Bell, how great a difference there is between their education and ours, especially from a religious point of view. Here was a young girl who had never entered a church or even seen one, had never conversed with a preacher or been approached upon the subject of the salvation of her soul, and never been told that there was any possible relation between her beliefs and conduct here, and her happiness or misery in a future existence.

The point which struck me was not the question of her religious beliefs, for while I have never asked her, yet from some words dropped in conversation I have reason to believe that she leans toward Spiritualism, but that which interested me was the fact, pure and simple, that her conduct was entirely free from religious influences.

We have no such characters among us, at least I have never seen any. We have unbelievers, agnostics, heathens even. The slums contain many youths who have never entered a church or attended Sabbath school, but still they have come in contact with men and women who go to both, and their conduct is influenced by what they hear from them. I doubt if any person can be found but what has heard of the Ten Commandments and know that they are held in reverence by persons that they themselves respect.

But not only this girl, but all these youths by whom I am surrounded, live in a country where there is no church, no Bible, no preachers, and where right and wrong are judged entirely upon the desirable or undesirable results of their actions.

What a different basis from our How flexible and open to change a nation thus educated must be, compared to one which is hampered by old traditions, and whose people respect and obey ancient laws, not because they fulfil any useful purpose, but because they are prefaced by a "Thus says the Lord."

How it simplifies the solution of the social problem to place it on a purely natural basis, by surrendering the belief that somewhere there resides a creator who has promulgated laws for the guidance of men, which are in direct opposition to the laws that control the balance of the Universe, and who compels obedience to these laws by rewards and punishments outside of the realm of natural results.

It brought strongly to my mind what Mr. Walter had told me on the boat, that they had adopted a standard of conduct in accord with the law of evolution, and which would greatly facilitate progress. As I get a better insight into the philosophy of these people, and learn to understand the beliefs which guide their conduct, I realize how difficult it will be for us to make any marked advance so long as we try to follow at the same time the teachings of the Bible and the dictates of our natural desires. We are a house divided against itself, and it

ANCIENT INSTITUTIONS. 69

helps us but little that our religious beliefs do not penetrate deeper than the surface, and our obedience to the Bible is more in form than reality.

The day after I had the conversation on education with Miss Bell was Sunday, and in the morning as I sauntered in the parlor after breakfast, she came to me and said: "You know, I suppose, Mr. Balcom, that this is a holiday with us. We cannot stop work entirely here, for there are many things which have to be done, but we suspend all but the most necessary occupations, and try to enjoy the day as much as possible. My work is such as can be laid aside for the day, and what little I have to do consists in helping those who are not so well favored. But I have most of the day free, and I would be pleased if you will come home with me and get acquainted with my parents."

Of course I gladly assented, and not long after we started to walk to their house. The streets were quiet, most all the stores closed, and the people whom we met were in their holiday attire. In the course of the conversation I remarked to Miss Bell that the absence of churches was something an American would be sure to notice.

"It is true that we have no churches in Socioland," she said, "and I have often wondered what people went to church for. Can you explain to me what is the attraction which takes them there?"

"Well, Miss Bell, I suppose it is habit more than anything else which takes people to church now. It is one of those duties which I told you of yesterday, that have been imposed upon us by the iron hand of spiritual authority. You may have heard that the Bible teaches that God created the world in six days and rested on the seventh, and on that account ordered that man should rest one day out of seven. Of course no one believes that now, but still the consecration of the seventh day to God's worship is upheld by men who believe one thing and preach another, and law and public opinion enforces it.

"Then some three thousand years ago, a Jewish king named Solomon built God a fine temple, for it was believed in those days that God took special pleasure in temples and had to be worshipped there. So in imitation of Solomon, Christians built churches everywhere and now, although they no longer believe in such a God, and no longer go to church to worship him, they go there to hear fine music, to listen or pretend to listen to a flowery discourse on subjects that have lost their interest for them, and to join in prayers which no longer come from the heart and are addressed to God, but are elaborate compositions pronounced for the entertainment of the congregation. And the force of habit is so great that churches are still built, and people found to attend them, although the belief which originally led to their construction and filled them with sincere, but ignorant worshippers, has been entirely outgrown.

"Do you understand now why it is so difficult to change our institutions? From the standpoint of Socioland there are no excuses for churches. The cost of their construction and the salaries of the preachers are useless expenses, for they do not contribute one iota to the public prosperity, or even preach a scientific code of morality.

"There would be some excuse if an honest religious belief was at the foundation of church-building and church-going, but that belief is nearly entirely gone. No educated person now believes in the six days' creation, or that God takes special pleasure in expensive buildings, or in fine organs, or in famous singers, and very, very few believe that to be a church member secures a passport to Paradise.

"No, it all rests upon inherited habits. It is the habit to

ANCIENT INSTITUTIONS. 71

uphold the churches, so they are upheld. It is the habit to say grace before meals, to open the sessions of legislatures with prayer, to grind the poor, to monopolize the land, to cheat the government, to settle all disputes by war, to spend millions upon the army, and so these things go on and no one dreams of changing them.

"But let any one propose something new, as for instance any legislation which might curtail the power of the rich and improve the condition of the poor, or promote a better distribution of the land, or reduce the expenses of the army and thus lighten the load on the shoulders of the workers, or a diminution in the number of the hours of labor, then an outcry is made by the conservative portion of society, for such dangerous demands were never made before, and if not promptly checked, the social edifice will be overthrown, and civilization buried under its ruins."

I stopped abruptly, for I recognized that I had got unduly excited, and I excused myself to Miss Bell. "I am afraid," I said, "that you will think me very uncourteous to allow such a digression to take up our time this pleasant morning, when agreeable thoughts alone ought to fill our minds. It was very wrong in me to indulge in such fault-finding, but I must acknowledge that I sometimes lose patience with these nominal Christians who are trying to save their souls and gain the whole world at the same time.

"What vexes me the most, Miss Bell, is that our best men and women, many of whom earnestly desire to see the social conditions improved, allow themselves to be turned aside from an honest study of the best solution of the problems involved, through fear that it might destroy the respect now entertained for these ancient institutions."

"I do not know," Miss Bell remarked, "that I correctly understand you. I can see that your people do many things that we would not think of doing, and you seem to think that they have no better reason for it except that it used to be thought the right thing in the past."

"Precisely so," I answered. "Thus if our ancestors had never gone to church, never observed the Sunday, the reasons now given would not be deemed sufficient to establish the custom. This matter of church-going is in itself of small importance, but it shows the tendency to hold on to old habits which prevents more important changes."

"Then, Mr. Balcom, the trouble seems to be in the conservative character of the people as much as in their religion."

"Yes and no. Not in the special religion, for the Buddhists and the Mahomeddans are yet more conservative than we are, but the influence of all so-called revealed religions is to chrystalyze the character and customs and thus prevent improvement.

"At the beginning, when first promulgated, they are a great force to impel forward civilization, but when their work is accomplished, and their strength has spent itself, they cannot be modified to suit the new conditions they themselves have helped to create, for they are supposed to come directly from God, so all the influence of their believers is exerted to prevent changes which would leave all their paraphernalia high, dry and useless. The more useful a religion has been in the past, the stronger is the hold it has taken upon the people, and the more difficult it is to hrow off the fetters it has placed upon its followers.

"But let us drop the subject, and now that I have told you about our national ideas upon keeping the Sunday, and why we go to church, please tell me how you spend the day here."

"Really, Mr. Balcom, there is very little to tell, for we have no special way of spending it, except as a day of rest and pleasure. It is the day of family gatherings, of feasts and picnics. We visit on that day more than upon any other, and public entertainments are provided for by the Townships, such as music in the parks, and dances. Those who are intellectually inclined can attend lectures and debates in our public halls, and we have also free excursions on the lake, rivers and railroads, although not very often on account of the extra work it gives to many persons who thus lose their chance of Sunday recreation. Every one spends his time as he chooses, and really the greatest difficulty is to select among the many pleasant ways provided for our amusement.

"But this is our house we are coming to, and I will have the pleasure of introducing you to my father and mother, and to the balance of the family."

CHAPTER XII.

HOUSEKEEPING IN SOCIOLAND.

Mr. Bell is a good-looking gentleman, yet in the prime of his strength and activity, and impressed me as possessing great will power and a sound judgment. He is heavily built, with a round head, keen gray eyes, a strong face, every lineament well defined. His wife is quick and impulsive, slender, with a refined face, and black hair and hazel eyes. They have two sons, one older and the other younger than their daughter. With the oldest one, a thriving young lawyer, I struck quite an acquaintance later on.

I was received very pleasantly by the family, and it seemed quite natural that the daughter should have invited me to spend the day at their house.

"We are very glad to see you, Mr. Balcom," Mrs. Bell said

to me after I had been introduced. "Mary has told us about you and how interested she is in all you tell her about the older countries. It is something new to her to hear about them, just as a great deal of what you see here must be new to you also."

I assented to her remarks, and thinking that it would be a good opportunity to learn something of the way in which their new institutions affected the female portion of the population, I turned the conversation in that direction by asking Mrs. Bell if they did not find it very difficult to hire house help in Socioland.

"Yes, of course," she answered. "It is not only difficult, but it is impossible here to have servants such as you are used to. Whoever we get to help us in the house we must treat as one of the family. Nobody would submit here to eat at a different table, receive their company in the kitchen, or sleep in a cupboard under the roof. You see our system of apprenticeship has a great influence upon the character of our girls. In the first place, the Commonwealth controls all their time from the age of fourteen until they are twenty. During that time these girls are much thrown together, often indeed dwell in the same house, eat at the same table, sleep in the same room, work in the same department, and associate in the same pleasures. It is not to be expected that girls so trained would be willing to accept a menial's position in a private family, especially as there are plenty of other occupations open to their choice, for everyone coming out of the training school is well fitted to earn her living in whatever direction she may prefer. There are girls who like to do house-work, and are willing to help in private families, but they must be treated as equals and not as servants, and we have to pay them as good a salary as they would earn as book-keepers or clerks in a store."

"That, Madam," I rejoined, "must be very pleasant for the girls, but cannot prove so satisfactory for those ladies who must either do their work without help, or must submit to close association with persons who may not be at all congenial to their tastes."

"I think that on the whole, Mr. Balcom, our system is preferable to yours, at least so far as I understand the way in which servants are treated in other countries. If idleness was the chief aim of woman, and happiness was reached by coming in daily contact with persons without education or culture, it would be different, but we would strongly object to bringing into our houses the class of persons on whom your women depend for the help they believe they must have. You may relegate your servants to the kitchen, and build back stairs for their especial use, and keep them at arm's length as much as possible, but the fact remains that they are a discordant element in the household, and while they may cater to the luxurious habits of your female population, it is not to be wondered at that there should be so much dissatisfaction as we hear exists with your servant system.

"Your women do not seem to look at this question in that light. They hire help to do their work, and if it is done in a satisfactory manner and at a reasonable price, they are willing to accept the annoyance of the daily contact as a necessary result.

"To us, who have never been used to the class from whom you draw your servants, for it does not exist here, the annoyance would be much greater, and I would never consent to bring into my home a person with whom I would be unwilling to associate on terms of equality."

"I know, Madam," I answered, "that there is much complaint at home about the servants. In the United States labor is so much better paid than in Europe, and so many more chances are open to the women to otherwise earn their living, that if it were not for the immigration, from the older countries, the supply would fall short of the demand. As it is, our help occupies a middle position between yours and that of Europe. We have many ladies who would prefer to do their work alone, but who find that they cannot stand it and at the same time keep their place in society. Their health and strength fails them, and they have to get help as a measure of self-preservation. How is it that you can manage it here, and are satisfied with all the burden of housekeeping resting upon you?"

"Mr. Balcom, the burden of housekeeping is largely what we make it ourselves, and if it is too heavy for us, it is usually our own fault. You will find that those ladies whose strength fails in doing their work, are trying to live in the same style as those who keep help. That is a pretty big undertaking, but there is worse yet. Your leaders in society not only have servants, but they have many more than they need, and are using their power in trying to outshine their less fortunate sisters, who, unwilling to be outdone, put out all their efforts to make what they call a respectable appearance. Is it surprising if they find it a hopeless struggle, and if they are compelled to hire help to enable them to make even a faint show of keeping up with the inflated style of living expected from all those who have some pretension to education and culture?

"We have got rid of that pernicious influence. We have no inordinately rich class to set up a false standard of life, no fashionable class to create useless wants and to inaugurate senseless fashions. Our fools—and I am sorry to say we have some yet among us—are in the minority, and instead of setting up for models, as with you, have to conform their conduct to that of the sensible portion of the community.

HOUSEKEEPING IN SOCIOLAND.

"You can't understand that this difference in our standard of living, which leads us to eschew all unnecessary display, is a great help to us. We aim to retain all the comfort possible, but those willing to live plainly can attain a great deal of comfort with a very reasonable amount of work. Besides, it is the policy of the Commonwealth to make life in Socioland as pleasant as possible, and the lightening of the labors of the women has not been forgotten in planning their public institutions. One of the most unpleasant features of housekeeping does not exist among us. I mean the washing and ironing of clothes. This is done free of charge by the Townships. In every Town there are public laundries where that work is done, and every week the cart comes around and takes away our soiled clothes and brings them back when clean. It is a great relief and a great saving of time, for it is a work which can be done much better and quicker in buildings which are fitted with proper mechanical appliances, than it can be done at home."

"I would have expected," I remarked, "to see such work done by private co-operation, but I find that the system does not meet with much favor with you."

"No, it does not," answered Mrs. Bell. "You see, co-operative laundries would only benefit a portion of the population, and cleanliness, which is said to be next to godliness, ought to be in reach of every one, especially of those who have the least time and money to spare. We have some co-operative enterprises, but the people do not seem ready to adopt the system in its closest relations where it would cause too much friction. We are making slow progress in that direction, and every year some families unite their fortunes and keep house together, but such experiments require for success special qualifications in character which are not yet common, although they are certainly increasing among us.

"But it is in public co-operation that we are succeeding best. For instance, by its help we have inaugurated a reform in visiting which has added to our leisure and enjoyment, and at the same time reduced our expenses and the labor of housekeeping. We have abolished the private parlor at home, and in its place the Towns have built Club houses where all our visiting is done. Instead of spending much time and money in keeping the best room ready to receive company, and having our time taken up in making or receiving calls, we see each other at the Club, where comfortable rooms are always open, and where we go whenever we feel disposed and can spare the time.

"This is comparatively a late innovation, and is the result of our peculiar condition. We found that we were drifting into a position where we must cease to visit at all except our most intimate friends, or let visiting take more of our time than was convenient under the circumstances. So we put our heads together, and after full discussion decided that the best remedy was for the Towns to erect buildings for social purposes, and very soon one was built for an experiment. The results were so satisfactory that now they are found all over the land, and formal calls are no longer known in Socioland. These Club houses are provided with comfortable parlors, music and reading rooms, and are open to all. They not only relieve us from the tediousness of formal calls, but furnish a pleasant place to spend a few hours, and help to keep up the social life among us.

"Thus you see, Mr. Balcom, that we have learned to relieve ourselves from too great a pressure at both ends of the social scale, and intend to make more progress in the same direction. The aims of the people have much to do with the march of improvement, and we must expect that ours will take a different course from what it has followed in other countries.

"In Europe, for instance, the rich have mastered the art of enjoying life, and of enhancing by all means in their power the pleasure of their existence, while all the efforts of the poor have been directed toward catering to that desire of the rich, so as to earn the necessary means to satisfy their own wants. The result has been that the genius and labor of that country have been turned in the direction of striving to please the taste and gratifying the whims of the owners of accumulated wealth. In your country, its immense resources have encouraged the creation and acquisition of wealth, and in that direction your powers are turned.

"Here our aims are changed. We have no rich class to cater to, nor any prospect of accumulating large amounts of wealth. It is not the individuals but the Commonwealth that is rich, and our efforts are directed to the increase of the comfort and happiness of all, women not excepted. Up to this time, the Commonwealth has had enough to do in placing within the reach of all its citizens those every-day comforts which in your land are the prerogative only of those who are said to be in easy circumstances, but we are fast increasing in public wealth, and expect soon to make further improvements which will make life still more pleasant and enjoyable.

"When that time comes, the claims of the women will not be forgotten, for here we are a political as well as a social power, and we have as much voice as the men in the management of the Commonwealth, but really I must say that we have little need to exert our influence, for the men are very considerate of us, and are always studying means by which they can make our tasks easier or our lives more pleasant."

Just then we were called to dinner by the younger brother, and adjourned to the next room where a plain meal was ready for us. Miss Mary and her brothers had quietly gone out of the room while we were talking and had set the table. We all sat around the board, and were soon engaged in a general conversation which was very interesting and lively, but which did not run on such topics as I have been writing to you, and on that account I will not try to reproduce it here.

CHAPTER XIII.

A TRUE COMMONWEALTH.

After dinner we adjourned to the garden, and soon Mr. Bell remarked that he judged from my conversation that I was interested in their public policy, and that if I wished he would explain some things which he thought might interest me. Of course I was glad to avail myself of such an opportunity, and expressed my willingness to hear whatever he might wish to say.

"The United States is a very rich country," he commenced, "but it cannot by any means be called a Commonwealth, for all the means of production are held in private hands, and very few or none are held in common. We believe in a true Commonwealth, and aim to make it rich so as to benefit the whole people. As wealth cannot be created by individual effort alone, but is the result of the combined industry of the whole people, it is but common justice that as far as possible the whole nation should profit by its increased production.

"As a result of your extreme individualism, you have no public wealth to be handed down from generation to generation, and the child of the poor man does not benefit in any

A TRUE COMMONWEALTH. 81

degree by the labor of his ancestors, for long before his birth all the valuable property in the country has passed into the hands of the capitalists, and he has to work just as hard to supply his wants as his parents did before him. The laborer draws his wages day by day, it is true, but the capitalist draws his interest, or his rent, or his profit, and besides reaps the whole benefit of the increased value of all investments, or what we call the unearned increment, which always follows the gradual improvement of the country.

"Such a condition of things is not just, and the philosophy on which it is based has been entirely repudiated by us. We believe it is both the protecting care of society, and the co-operation of capital and labor which makes this unearned increment possible, and that the whole Commonwealth ought to profit by it as far as conditions permit.

"And now let me explain to you how we went to work to establish what we consider a true Commonwealth.

"The founders of Socioland, as you know, came from the United States. They had seen in less than two centuries the whole wealth of the nation pass into the hands of a privileged class. The land was held by a few while multitudes were homeless; gold and silver mines yielded their riches into the hands of a few millionaires, who conjointly with the money-kings controlled the financial policy of the nation; the coal mines were in the hands of monopolists who checked the output so as to create an artificial scarcity; the railroads, instead of being managed in the interests of the people, were manipulated for purposes of speculation, or combined so as to prevent competition. Everywhere, private individuals, either singly, or banded in limited numbers, were striving to accumulate fortunes by compelling the consumer to pay them tribute, and using all lawful means to give fictitious value to the property in their hands.

"These results were not due to any of the causes from which the oppressed peoples of Europe had suffered. There was no aristocracy with vested rights, no kings to give away the people's substance to court favorites, no standing army to prey on the wealth of the nation. They were the outcome of perfect freedom in competition, and of the policy which had thrown open to all comers the chances of taking and keeping possession of all the means of production. Individualism in economics had run mad, and the weakest members of society had been crowded to the wall in the unequal struggle.

"Our predecessors decided rightly that they would provide against such results here, and that measures should be taken to prevent the monopoly by individuals of the means of production.

"The first thing to be done was to create a fund which would enable the Commonwealth to carry on its own business enterprises. That was not an easy undertaking, for when they came here they brought but little wealth with them, and what they did bring was private property. The Commonwealth could, of course, have taxed some of that property, or it could have borrowed it, but either course would have been opposed to the policy they wanted to inaugurate. Taxation in any form is always objectionable, and borrowing is worse, for none can lend but the rich, and it is placing a mortgage upon the labor of the country for their benefit. Both borrowing and taxation are crude methods practised by nations ignorant of the laws which ought to control social interests, and would long ago have been abolished, were it not that through their agency the rich contrive to throw all the financial burdens on those who labor.

"No, the first settlers managed the business of the Commonwealth precisely as a wise young man starting in life would have managed his own. They husbanded their resources, and

A TRUE COMMONWEALTH. 83

kept their expenses below their receipts. The first money which came into their hands was made by providing the people with a medium of exchange. Treasury notes were issued and made a legal tender for all debts, and no other money was recognized as having a legal existence. Then the land was thrown open for settlement, and rights of occupancy sold which helped to fill the Treasury.

"With the funds thus secured, the Commonwealth started the wholesale trade and the business of common carrier. Of course it was slow work at first, but it was for the common interest to see the public fund increase and prosper, and by good management and economy the profits accumulated till ample means were provided for all public enterprises.

"Yet it took nearly twenty-five years before the Commonwealth felt rich enough to commence repaying to its citizens the returns secured by their abstinence, but now that we are receiving the full benefits accrued to us by the wise policy of our parents, we can bless them for the rich inheritance they have secured to us. They have planted the seed, and it has grown and prospered, and every year it gives us a plentiful harvest.

"Now, Mr. Balcom, if you will tell me what is the amount of taxation in the United States, I will try and show you the difference it makes to the working people between our policy and yours."

"I cannot tell you positively," I answered, "for we have city, county, state and federal taxes, and they are levied in so many different ways that there are no means of learning the exact amount of our taxation, but I suppose that each person must contribute at least twenty dollars a year to support our different governments."

"Taking your estimate as proximately correct," continued Mr. Bell, "and if there is one able-bodied man to every four persons, we find that each one has to produce eighty dollars a year to help pay public expenses.

"Here we have no taxes at all. Instead the Commonwealth has an income over and above all expenses of twenty-five dollars to each person, or one hundred dollars to each ablebodied man.

"We have now here about one million inhabitants, and our surplus income is over twenty-five million dollars, earned in our import and export and wholesale trade, our transportation agencies and our insurance policies. As the Commonwealth has accumulated over four hundred million dollars of capital, you can see that our surplus income only represents a fair interest on the capital invested, and not one cent for profit.

"This income, earned in common, is spent for the common good and in promoting the comfort of all. A large proportion is re-invested every year in improvements calculated to increase the producive power of the Commonwealth, and in developing its natural resources. What in your land is left to private enterprise, acting purely from selfish impulses, and regardless of the best interests of the nation, is done by us under the broader principle of a wise and scientific development of our producing power, and no money is spent in permanent improvements until a thorough scientific investigation has been made to see that they co-ordinate with the plans which have been previously decided upon as offering the best prospect of promoting public success. The industrial development of Socioland bears to that of the United States the same relation that the systematic drainage of a large tract of land would bear to the drainage of the same land by a number of individuals or private corporations, each working for private advantage and in competition with the interest of others.

"Besides the capital we thus invest each year, a large amount of our surplus earnings is spent for the direct comfort of the

A TRUE COMMONWEALTH.

people. It is now over one half, and as our producing power increases, the proportion we can thus spend will increase also.

"My wife told you about our public laundries and our Club houses, and you have seen our parks and know of our schools, but you may not know that the bread cart furnishes to all the citizens, free of cost, all the bread they wish to consume, or that both gas and water are free in every house, or that we pension the aged and the needy, and have free hospitals and asylums.

"Thus you see, Mr. Balcom, we have reason to congratulate ourselves upon the results of the policy inaugurated by the founders of Socioland, but there is another advantage which it is difficult to estimate in dollars and cents, and yet which must not be forgotten. It is the great reduction in the price of all necessaries of life. A reduction which has not been effected by forcing down the wages of the working men, but by eliminating from our Commonwealth all methods through which one class of people can live at the expense of the other. Rent, interest and profit are kept within reasonable bounds and the heavy load they place on the shoulders of labor has almost disappeared.

"You can see now the difference in the prospects of a child who is born here and one born in other countries. If born in the United States, as soon as he commences to produce, he will be taxed eighty dollars a year to maintain the government, and in return has been educated at public expense, and will be protected in his civil and political rights. The country he is ushered into has long ago passed into the hands of individuals or corporations who look upon such as he as tools in their hands to increase their wealth. His predecessors, instead of saving and investing property, borrowed money and left it as a mortgage on his work in the form of a public debt.

"Of Commonwealth there is none, and while there is a large

amount of producive capital, it is all in private hands, and the child of poor parents has little to be thankful for that his lot in life has fallen in what is called a civilized country for all that which makes life desirable is already appropriated, and his education only makes more galling the load he has to bear.

"Here the child finds himself in entirely different conditions. No taxes to pay, no idle class to support, no monopolies to levy tolls on his labor. Instead a well-invested public fund of four hundred million dollars, of which he is a share-holder, and which will help him to raise himself to the position his natural capacities enable him to occupy. It will not destroy his incentive to improvement, or make him the equal of his fellow-citizens, but it will insure him a standing place in the community, from which he can raise himself as high as his abilities will allow him.

"All these results are attained without curtailing individual enterprise, or preventing any one from getting all the property they can use to their advantage, or which is necessary to minister to their comfort. It is simply due to a policy which prevents the monopoly of natural resources, and the excessive accumulation of wealth in private hands."

I have here, my dear Harry, given you more the substance than the form of our conversation, for we spoke of many other things, and the ladies were not so entirely left out as my account would make it appear, for in this advanced state the women are interested in public affairs, and not only vote, but hold positions of trust. But the conversation was mostly carried on by Mr. Bell, his wife and children having a natural respect for his opinions, and allowing him to explain the working of their institutions, only occasionally putting in a remark here and there.

CHAPTER XIV.

A PLEASANT RIDE.

Toward the middle of the afternoon Miss Bell proposed that, if I thought I would enjoy it, we take a ride to the park and out in the suburbs of the Town.

Of course such an offer was not to be refused, and as Mr. Bell keeps a very neat turnout, not a long space of time elapsed till I found myself seated at her side.

Miss Bell held the reins, and turning to me said: "I have offered to take you to the park, Mr. Balcom, but if you prefer it we can drive some other way."

"No, Miss Mary," I answered. "I place myself in your hands and I am sure I shall enjoy myself wherever we go."

"Then if you leave it with me," said Miss Bell, "I will first take you to the park that you may see how we enjoy ourselves, and after we will drive out in the country."

So we drove along the street where Mr. Bell lives, and soon reached the river on which Spencer is built. The park, situated on that river, is very large and is left quite wild. Except at the entrance, where a portion is laid out in walks and drives, and ornamented with lawns and flowers, it has been left almost entirely in its natural state, except that roads and paths have been cut in available places, and rough benches and tables constructed for the convenience of the picnickers.

The park contains also a large music stand with a dancing floor attached to it, where a merry and noisy crowd was enjoying itself heartily. Merry-go-rounds, swings, shooting galleries and all the many amusements usually found at fairs were there in abundance, and the whole place seemed to be given up to harmless enjoyment.

The woods and lawns were full of pleasure parties, many seeming to have spent the day there, having set up their croquets and hammocks, and otherwise having made themselves entirely at home.

After taking in the sights in the park, we struck out for the country on a road skirting the river. The day was beautiful, the air had become cool, and as we sped along at a fine rate I found my position very pleasant, and as I leaned back on my seat, thinking of all I had heard and seen since my arrival in Spencer, I seemed to realize more and more the advantages enjoyed by the people of this favored Commonwealth, and turning to my companion, I said to her:

"Miss Mary, you must be very happy here, for your position in life is pleasant indeed, and you live in a community where the people certainly possess the art of enjoying themselves."

Miss Bell paused a moment before answering, seeming to be in deep thought, but finally remarked. "Yes my life is very happy, but really I have never given the subject much thought. You see our days flow on so evenly that we enjoy our happiness as a matter of course. All our lives are pleasant here, mine no more than those of the people with whom I live."

"But Miss Bell," I remarked, "has all your life been happy? Did you not have an unpleasant time when you left your home and went to live among strangers? Please tell me a little about your early life and your school days."

"There is really very little to tell, Mr. Balcom. I think here every one is kind to children and tries to make them happy. My earliest recollections are of the pleasant time I had with my parents while yet a little girl, of long walks and rides, of helping mother in the lightest tasks of house-work, and of how proud I was when I could feel that I had been of some use. Then my parents helped me to learn how to read and write, and I soon appreciated the pleasure I received from study, so as I grew older and began to understand the advantages of knowledge, I was eager enough to get all the information within my reach.

"I never went to school until I was ten years of age, and by that time I had acquired with a little help from my parents the rudiments of an English education, and had gone as far as I could without teachers. So I was glad to receive help from competent persons who had ample time to devote to me. In school I found myself among children of my age or older, who were also interested in their studies and needed no urging from their teachers. Yes indeed, those were pleasant days when we commenced to drink deep at the fountain of knowledge, and our minds began to appreciate the beauties and wonders of nature. Botany, astronomy, chemistry, physic, history, geography, were taught to us, and we liked our studies so well that the time seemed far too short for all we wanted to learn."

"But," I remarked, "were not those interesting studies mixed with some not so pleasant? What about many subjects which are not supposed to have much interest for young girls, but which they must learn if they want to be thoroughly educated?"

"Of course, Mr. Balcom, all studies did not have the same interest for us, but we never were requested to learn what we did not want to. For instance, if a scholar did not wish to study arithmetic, the teacher would explain to him its use, and how much he would need it in his work, but no effort would be made to compel him, and if he could not see that it would be for his advantage to study it, the teacher would simply tell him that he was the one to decide, for if a mistake was made he would be the one to suffer from it.

"Some special studies, as geometry and algebra were only

undertaken by those who had a taste for them, and teachers were provided for those who had a taste for artistic pursuits.

"And thus the few years that were spent at school passed all too quickly, and left a very pleasant impression behind."

"From what you tell me," I said, "I judge that the same difference exists between the methods of education here and ours, as exists between all our public institutions. With us, scholars are made to study, whether interested or not, and no efforts are made to teach them the benefits that will follow from their education, except that it is the usual and proper course to take for children in their social position. You, on the other hand, induce the children to study by helping them to increase their knowledge of those things which interest them, and by explaining to them the help they will receive in their future carreers from the knowledge that is placed within their reach."

"I do not know how it is in other countries," replied Miss Bell, "but I know that in Socioland very litte compulsion is ever used. We are told that if we desire to attain certain ends, certain means must be used, and we are left free to use those means or neglect them as we choose. But let me assure you that very few of us neglect them, and that the spirit of improvement and the desire to learn are so strong that our teachers are more anxious to restrain than to urge. On that account the hours of study are short, and as much out of door exercises intermingled as possible. Many studies are taught in pleasant talks in the open air, and short lectures given us in our rambles."

"I think I have been told, Miss Bell, that the time of apprenticeship for girls commences in their fourteenth year. If that is the case, your school days are soon over. You have but four years, if I count right?"

"Yes, you are right, and then we enter into an entirely

different, but not unpleasant life. We are expected at that time to have arrived at an age when we can appreciate the need of work, and the necessity that we should fit ourselves for the battle of life. We are taught while at school, that all the advantages we enjoy here are the result of man's and woman's labor, and that incessant care is needed for their maintenance, and we are impressed with the fact that when old enough we shall be enrolled in the army of workers who are engaged in maintaining and increasing the welfare of the Commonwealth. Thus we are led to realize that we will in our turn become useful members of society.

"It is with those feelings that we enter upon our term of apprenticeship, and we are proud of the trust which is placed in us. When I was fourteen my name was enrolled among the apprentices, and I was directed to make my choice between the vacant places offered by the different Managers. The two first years we are requested to do housework, and to commence with the most simple and easy occupations, so I entered in the hotel where I am now, and made myself useful in the housekeeping department. But except that I had to live away from home there was nothing unpleasant about it. The work was light, for there is always an abundance of help, and I had many hours I could devote to study. I have some taste for music, and could find all the time I wanted to practice, and had good teachers to help me along.

"At the end of two years I was allowed to make my choice of the kind of occupation I wanted to perfect myself in, and as my taste led me more toward office work than to housekeeping, I devoted less time to my house duties and commenced to learn short-hand, type-writing and book-keeping, and was set to work in the office. As other girls left, I had more work put under my charge, so that now I have all the correspondence and most of the books under my supervision. It is work I like, I have all the help I need, all the leisure I can enjoy, and you see I have good reasons to be satisfied."

"But, Miss Bell," I said, "this will not last. In one year from now all that will be changed. You will be through with your term of apprenticeship and you will have to leave the hotel, for I do not suppose that Mr. Wilton can afford to keep you when he will have to pay you a salary."

"I do not know, Mr. Balcom, what I shall do when that time comes. Our motto here is, 'Care not for the morrow, for sufficient unto the day is the Good thereof,' but I know that if it does not suit Mr. Wilton to keep me, I can find plenty of occupations to choose from. I may get married, or I can return home and help mother, or start in business for myself, or find employment in some public or private office. Oh! no, we are never troubled with lack of opportunities here, the difficulty is all the other way, to select from the many openings offered to us."

"I suppose, Miss Mary, that the same liberty is given to all in selecting a vocation?"

"Certainly, all have the same liberty, but all, boys and girls, are required to start at the bottom of the industrial scale, and to stay there some time too. They run errands, help the older persons, and learn the A. B. C. of the industrial alphabet. But as new recruits come in, they are promoted, until having mastered the rudiments of industrial knowledge, they are allowed to select the special branch in which they wish to perfect themselves, and places are found for them according to their desires.

"Had I desired to learn housekeeping, I would have been put in charge of some minor departments, and gradually promoted to the higher ones. If I had selected teaching, a place would have been found for me in the schools. Whatever we choose, we are helped to make it a success, but no compulsion is ever used, and we are left free to decide for ourselves the occupation in which we desire to improve our opportunities."

"Yes! yes! I see." I could not help saying. "You rely upon kindness and intelligence. You instruct your young people in the construction of society, and show them the relation which exists between useful knowledge and success and happiness. Our children have no such teachings, and most of them are led to believe that their success or failure will depend on a lucky or unlucky chance. Very few of our youths have any idea of the relation which exists between their education and their success in life. Education is accepted by most of them as one of the requirements of their position, and not as a means to a well-defined end.

"Of course many of them, as their minds mature, see that it is a mistake and commence to study with an intelligent purpose, but they are left to make the discovery for themselves, and the majority of our boys and girls never find it out, and only study because they are made to, and because it is the proper thing in the class to which they belong."

Our conversation after this drifted away from that subject, and after a very pleasant ride of several miles through a rich and well cultivated country, we returned to the city, and I was kindly invited by the family to spend the evening with them.

CHAPTER XV.

THE LAND QUESTION.

You know, my dear Harry, that among the many social questions which influence the welfare of humanity, there is none of more importance, or which at this time has been more discussed, than the ownership of land.

The absolute ownership of the soil, as enforced in Europe and America, has given rise to so many abuses, has enabled individuals and corporations to get possession of such vast tracts, and to ask such enormous prices for desirable parcels of land, that it is everywhere recognized as one of the great factors in the inequality of wealth, and a great impediment to the equitable distribution of products.

On the other hand it is argued by the conservative members of society, that the absolute ownership of land by the individuals is necessary for the best improvement of the soil, and that unless owners are certain of reaping the benefits of their labors, they will only skim the surface and spend neither time nor money in those improvements which must be made if the country is to attain its highest development.

You are as familiar as I with all the arguments, pro. and con., of this momentous question, as well as with the many schemes which have been proposed to reconcile the interests involved.

I was aware, from what Mr. Walter had told me, that they had a somewhat different land tenure in Socioland from that which obtains with us, and I was glad of the opportunity offered by an evening spent with Mr. Bell to get some information from him on the subject. I feel that he is a clear-headed, well-informed man, whose opinions ought to have weight, and who would not willingly color any statement he should make. So I took the first convenient occasion to broach the subject.

"This land question," he said, "is one of the most difficult we had to contend with, and we cannot claim to have settled it yet, nor is it likely to be settled for ages to come. Nothing short of a state of perfect millenium, a time when production will have become so large as to supply all possible wants, and when centuries of peace and prosperity will have so softened all hearts, and so bound men together as to destroy the incentive to private interests, will enable men to reconcile public and private claims to the ownership of land.

"But if we have not reached that stage, I believe we have made some advance, and our system, if still open to objections, is yet greatly preferable to that which obtains in other countries.

"I could in a few words explain to you what our system is, but I think you will understand us better if I go back a little and explain to you our position from the beginning. It will take a little more time, but it will be more satisfactory in the end."

I signified my assent and Mr. Bell continued:

"The foundation of our system was established before my time, but the traditions of the first settlement of the country were part of my early education, and if I did not participate in the events of those days, I lived on terms of intimacy with those who took an active part in the decisions of those times

"Our predecessors had seen enough in the United States to make them keenly alive to the evils of private ownership of land, and they decided unanimously that the Commonwealth would retain for ever the control of the land, but that all persons who desired to settle and improve some of it, should be allowed to acquire a right of occupancy to a vacant tract, and that this right should hold good against all private interests, but should be forfeited to the Commonwealth upon the payment of actual damages, whenever the land was needed for public purposes.

"After so much had been decided upon, the next question which presented itself was this: Should this right be a free gift or should it be paid for? Should it be for a limited or unlimited number of acres? These questions were soon forced upon the new community. When the site for the city of Spencer had been decided upon, there soon manifested itself a natural desire from each one to possess as well-located and as large a tract as possible. On the other hand, the Commonwealth needed money, and was anxious to secure funds without resorting to taxation.

"The result of these contending forces was that, after special tracts had been reserved for public use, the land was divided into zones, commencing at the centre of the city. In the inner zone no one could occupy more than one acre, in the next zone the limit was placed at five acres, in the next at ten acres, while it was decided that thirty acres for one person, or sixty for a married couple, would be the largest tract granted, even at the furthest extremity of the Comonwealth, and taking in consideration the public need of money, and the desire that all should have the same chance to the land of their choice, it was decided unanimously to sell the tracts at auction."

"And did the plan succeed?" I asked, "and is the public satisfied, and does it still regulate the ownership of the soil?"

"Yes," answered Mr. Bell. "It proved in the main satisfactory, and not nearly as liable to abuse as the old system. The plan is the same, but we have reduced the size of the lots to suit the needs of our increased population, for you know that we claim that it is one of the advantages of our institutions that we can change our policy to suit the needs of the times.

"No changes were needed for many years, but as the country became settled, small business centers began to grow in many directions, and new Townships had to be established, and thus new and independent zones had to be marked out. At the sites selected for the business locations of these new Townships, many persons had to be dispossessed of their rights because the land was needed for public use. They were repaid the money they had paid at first, and were compensated for the improvements they could not remove. Of course it was not pleasant, but as their neighbors had to reduce the size of their holdings, they were enabled to make satisfactory purchases, and the increased prosperity of the whole settlement was a full compensation to all the parties for their trouble."

"And here in Spencer itself, I suppose you found it necessary to make some changes?"

"Oh! yes, we had to make them also. The Town had to take back some of the land it had sold, and in the center of the city the limit has been cut down to half an acre, while the limits of the acre zone have been much extended."

"But do not these enforced changes create much disturbance?" I asked. "I represent to myself what a commotion it would create among us if such an order was enforced."

"You would find," Mr. Bell answered, "that it would only affect the very rich in your large cities, for the high price of your land brings about the same results. With you the division of the soil is fostered by its increased value, which makes it more profitable for the owner to sell than to hold it. With us it is different. Our system of land tenure destroys speculation and prevents high prices, so we must resort to other means to compel its division. And we find our policy answer very well our purpose.

"Those who have acquired rights of occupancy in a growing city, know that they will some day have to divide with others, and act accordingly. Many a father gives his children a portion of his land who would have held on to it till death released his grip. Many a person sells at a reasonable price a piece of land to the man who needs it, who would have taken advantage of his power to drain him of his last possible dollar.

"Besides we give plenty of time for the changes to take place easily and gradually. Our citizens are more induced than compelled to divide with those in need. When the land within the acre limit had been practically all occupied, there were found many persons willing to pay the occupants a fair price for a part of their lots, and the persons in possession, knowing that eventually they would be compelled to sell, were inclined to make a virtue of necessity, and part with what they otherwise might have preferred to keep.

"Mark you, nothing is taken which is necessary to the possessor's comfort and welfare. The size of the lots is always ample for all legitimate wants. It is only the superfluous they are compelled to give up, and the sense of insecurity it gives in the possession of the superfluous is an important factor in inducing our people to divide with those who are less favored.

"You must have noticed, Mr. Balcom, that our aims are entirely different from yours. You are after stability, you are afraid of changes, you dread the weakening of the existing order of society. We care nothing for these things. We are trying to improve our condition in life, and are ready to change every day if we are better satisfied thereby. That which we want to see enduring is not the institutions, but the happiness of the community.

THE LAND QUESTION.

"But to return to the land question. As population increases, the tendency is to an amiable division of the property, as preferable to an enforced one, which is sure to come sooner or later. When this process has been going on for a sufficient length of time to allow all right minded persons to adjust the size of their lots to the public welfare, a vote is taken and two or three years given for the enforced reduction of the holdings to the new limit, after which the occupants lose their rights to the excess of their property which reverts back to the Commonwealth without compensation."

"And how," I asked, "does your policy affect the general settlement of the country?"

"Our country has been surveyed, the best locations for railroads and public roads decided upon, which are built as fast as needed, and we settle the country as we go, avoiding premature expenses and needless privations.

"We are in no hurry to develop all our resources at once, for we have nothing to gain by it. We do not, as is the case with you, build long lines of railroads going through deserts and uninhabited countries, to carry settlers from rich farming sections only half cultivated, to far-off states just opened to civilization. It is private speculation which induces your people to this course, and engenders the desire to get possession of large tracts of land, but the result is an immense amount of wasted labor and needless hardships.

"Your system of land ownership is suited to the ideas and character of your people, and fosters the spirit of enterprise which is fast making the United States the richest nation in the world. Our system is suited to our character and aims. We do not develop as fast, but we avoid the evil of land speculation and monopoly of the soil. Yours is the hot-bed growth, fostered by the desire for riches, ours is the healthier growth of a contented people, following the line of intelligent development.

"And what about the titles to these rights?" I asked. "Do you have the same system of transfer by deeds as obtains in other countries?"

"No, we have not, and thus we have done away with a fruitful source of litigation. The Townships alone can grant those rights of occupancy or transfer them. Whenever a change is made, the former occupant relinquishes his right, which is cancelled, and a new one is issued. Transfer by inheritance follows the same rule. And the change once made is final and not to be disturbed or questioned, for we hold that it is of the utmost importance that the men who labor on the soil should feel all possible security, and that improvement and occupancy are worthy of more consideration than ancient deeds or mislaid wills.

"Many of the results of our land policy may seem hard and arbitrary to those who are used to the absolute ownership of the soil, and to the right of sale and mortgage, but to us who have never been used to them, we look only to the results on the public prosperity, and they are eminently satisfactory.

"No public enterprise is thwarted by the selfishness or stubbornness of individuals or corporations, no large tracts monopolized by shrewd speculators, no exorbitant ground rents levied on commerce or manufactures, no endless and expensive litigation entered into because some lost marriage certificate has been found, or a flaw discovered to invalidate some ancient title.

"It might be thought that the feeling of insecurity to individuals would more than offset those advantages, but we do not find it so, for sudden changes are never made, and they are always the result of the best judgment of the people, publicly discussed and expressed, and always directed toward increasing the prosperity of the community.

"Besides the tendency of our institutions is such that while it checks the large accumulation of wealth in the hands of those of a grasping disposition, it also checks the tendency to waste of the property held by those who are inclined to be reckless or extravagant, so that on the whole there are probably less changes in the occupancy of the soil in Socioland, than there is to be found under the absolute ownership of other countries."

About that time the ladies came in, and after a pleasant social evening, I walked back to the hotel with Miss Bell, well satisfied with the way in which the day had been spent.

CHAPTER XVI.

ARBITRATION AND LAWS.

I believe I told you before, my dear Harry, that I had found an agreeable friend in William Bell, the older brother of Miss Mary. He is a bright young man, very enthusiastic as to the future of Socioland, and thoroughly imbued with the spirit which prevails here.

He is a lawyer by profession, but the word has an entirely different meaning here from that which we give it, or it would be more correct to say that it means here what our best lawyers are and what they all ought to be. Instead of fomenting trouble and fostering lawsuits, their work consists in settling differences and adjusting difficulties, and in presenting their client's case clearly and concisely to the judge when their efforts do not meet with success. They act more as counsellors and advisers than as advocates, and in fact I find that the law has much less to do here than with us, in regulating the relations of men to each other.

As I have plenty of time, I often drop in his office, and if I find him at leisure we drift in conversation upon all kinds of subjects, and I think it will interest you if I repeat some of our talks upon their ideas of law and government.

I was telling him a few days ago that, as far as I knew, there had been only two forms of government tried. One was the autocratic, where the rulers had succeeded in obtaining control of the power and were using it to their own advantage, and the other the representative form, where the people try to govern themselves by delegating their powers to legislative bodies who make the laws and provide means to enforce them. But I said that it seemed to me that here in Socioland they were experimenting on a third method, where the people tried to govern themselves with as little intervention of delegates as possible.

"Yes," he answered. "Our system is peculiar to ourselves, and is the result of the philosophical beliefs of those who founded our Commonwealth, and of the conditions under which it has been started.

"I have," he further remarked, "read extensively about the laws and customs of other nations, and I find that the constant trend of the oppressed has been to have justice meted out to them, and to gain possession of what they consider their rights. In the pursuit of these aims they have elaborated constitutions defining the relations of men to each other, and enacted numberless laws to compel due respect for these rights in order that justice might be maintained.

"Now we look upon these ideas as entirely natural for those who are oppressed and at the same time are taught that God has created all men equal; but for us who have eliminated all forms of oppression from among us as inimical

ARBITRATION AND LAWS. 103

to happiness, and believe in the evolution of man from a lower organism, and in the struggle for existence and the survival of the fittest, such a view is entirely unscientific, and cannot furnish a sound basis for the forming of constitutions or the enactment of laws."

"What!" I said. "Do you not believe in the need of justice or the enforcement of rights?"

"No, not in the sense in which you use these words," he answered. "With us they only mean a form of conduct which experience has shown to be beneficent to mankind, and calculated to promote the best interests of society. But we do not believe that in the light of the evolution theory there can be such a thing in nature as abstract justice, or that it is possible to attain perfect rights.

"In your search after this ignis-fatuus you are all the time trampling upon justice and violating natural rights. Like the man who loved peace so well that he was always willing to fight to attain it, you are all the time unconsciously breaking the very principles you are trying to establish. For instance what greater violation of natural rights can there be than the individual appropriation of land? By what right, please tell me, can any man or a body of men say of a portion of the soil: 'This is mine.' They did not create it. It was there long before them, and will remain long after they have passed away. And yet habit has so blunted your sense of right that you talk about the natural right of men to their land, as if they had an actual right to it instead of having only a legal title to it, based originally upon spoliation and force.

"And talk about justice. Is it just, tell me, to take a husband and father from his family, and send him to fight the battles of his country because he happens to be under a certain age, while an older man, with as much or more at stake is allowed to remain at home? Is there any justice in preventing a man from voting until he is twenty-one years of age, or in keeping a woman away from the polls altogether?

"Go to Europe, to America, to Socioland, or to any country, and you will find that perfect justice does not exist, cannot exist in fact, for it is not in accord with the law of evolution, and all the efforts of mankind do not enable them to attain it."

To this tirade I could make no reply, for it was a new idea to me, and one I had never studied, so I confined myself to asking my friend if they were going to do without justice, by what did they intend to replace it?

"Those were the views entertained by the first settlers," he answered, "so instead of seeking the establishment of justice and the maintenance of individual rights, they sought to promote a spirit of friendliness and good-will toward all, and shaped their laws so as to discourage litigation, and to induce the people to settle their differences among themselves. They abandoned the jury system as too expensive and cumbrous, and abolished the right of appeal to higher courts. The decision of the judge is final and must be accepted as such.

"You believe that the enforcement of justice is the duty of the government, and that you must see to it that every man is protected in his natural rights. We look upon the men who cannot agree among themselves as undesirable citizens, and we only settle their disputes for them because it is the best way for the peace and happiness of the community. But it must be done quickly, and at the least possible expense of time and money. If the parties do not like the judge's decision, they will be more inclined to come to a mutual understanding next time, or to resort to arbitration, which we favor by all means in our power.

"The law has very little to say about the enforcement of contracts or the collection of debts, for we think it better to

ARBITRATION AND LAWS. 105

teach our people that they must look to the honesty of the contracting parties, than to the help of the Commonwealth for the fulfilment of promises made. Suits for damages are discouraged, for we think it best to live down slander than to intensify it by ventilating it before the public. In civil suits, the statute of limitation promptly debars the complainant, for we hold that differences ought to be quickly settled and quickly forgotten, nor do we have sufficient respect for the dictates of the dead to allow mislaid wills to disturb existing conditions.

"Besides, we leave the individuals much freer to control their private actions than is done in other countries. We do not try to make the people religious or moral by law. Marriage and divorce are free, religious convictions are never interfered with, all days are equal before the law, and all personal actions are left as much as possible to be controlled by the intelligent judgment of the individuals concerned.

"Criminal cases are treated differently. They are rare with us, because we have done away with the incentives to crime, but when they do occur, we look upon the culprits as diseased persons and treat them accordingly.

"To all these changes the objection might be made that justice must often suffer, and if perfect justice was our aim, we would certainly be advancing in the wrong direction. But we do not believe that perfect justice can be attained, and we know that it is daily violated, even by those nations who have the most elaborate code of laws. So we prefer to look to the culture of kindly feelings and to the increase of community of interests for the recognition of as many individual rights and the establishment of as much justice as the social conditions permit.

"It is by thus diminishing the number of the laws, and teaching the people the art of individual control, that we can govern ourselves by direct legislation, and take from our legislative bodies the power they so often abuse in representative countries, and I believe our people get along as well or better than those nations who look for the proper regulation of individual conduct to the increase in number of their laws."

And it is true that the people of Spencer seem remarkably well behaved. Bar-rooms are unknown, and drunkenness does not seem to exist here, and no loafers are to be met on the street corners. When I asked my friend how they had succeeded in banishing these pests of civilized countries, he said he did not know how it was brought about, for he had never seen them and he did not believe the species existed in Socioland or had been imported there. He supposed the climate was not favorable to that kind of growth, for though once in a while disreputable characters made their appearance on the streets, they looked so lost and forlorn, and so quickly disappeared from the public gaze, that probably they mended their ways or left in search of more congenial climes.

A few days later, my friend gave me an interesting account of the formation of their government as he had heard it from the first settlers.

"I was told" he said, "that when the first emigrants arrived here, they decided, contrary to all precedents, to draft no constitution, to enact no laws, but to wait and decide each case as it presented itself. They were not numerous then, and used to meet in a large hall, which was one of the first buildings they put up, and talk matters over and decide what course they had better follow. These decisions, duly recorded and voted upon, are the foundation of all our laws, but are liable to modification by popular vote at any time.

"Our business system was organized in the same way, and by the same process our first Managers were appointed. When the time arrived for the Commonwealth to commence business

ARBITRATION AND LAWS.

on its own account, the best men were selected to take it in charge and do the best they could for the community. 'How long shall we serve?' they asked. 'As long as you give satisfaction,' we answered.

"The experiment was a success. These men took pride in their work and spared no efforts to make it successful. It was found best to give them much latitude of action and to appoint Advisory Boards to help them co-ordinate their efforts.

"When the first disagreement among the settlers arose, there was no court, jury or judge, so a reliable man was selected to settle their dispute, and it was decided to enforce his decision whatever it might be, and thus our first judge was created.

"For several years there was no legislature, for the people met in mass-meetings to discuss and vote upon such questions as presented themselves, and at this time all our Townships are thus governed till the increase of population makes it impracticable. But our legislative bodies have none of the power they possess in other countries, and only act as committees where the different opinions are discussed and condensed, and finally put in shape to be voted upon by the people.

"Our system is not at all calculated to promote extensive legislation, and if we were a law-making and a law-loving people, we would not be satisfied with it. But we look upon law at best as a necessary evil, and replace it as far as possible by conciliation and kindly feelings."

CHAPTER XVII.

THE CONDITIONS OF SUCCESS.

I have not said anything to you about Mr. Walter, although I have seen him often, and called upon him several times at his house, because I have tried to confine myself as far as possible to the topics and conversations which treat more specially of the public institutions of Socioland. But I will give you an account of the last conversation I had with him, for I think it will interest you to know his views upon the diffusion of the principles they advocate, and their adoption by other countries.

I had been calling upon him, and seated in his library he addressed me thus:

"Well, my young friend, you have been here some little time, and must have formed some opinions as to what you have seen, and must understand the results of the changes we have made in our form of government. How does it strike you? Have we progressed, or have we been taking backward steps in civilization?"

"I must say," I answered, "that it seems to me that you have made great progress, and have established here a Commonwealth from which you have eliminated many of the defects which still exist in other countries, and I would be pleased indeed if some of the changes you have inaugurated here could also be made in the United States. It would go very far to ameliorate the condition of the lower classes, and increase the comfort and happiness of the whole people."

"Yes, those changes are desirable, or at least we think so here, or we would not have instituted them," he answered.

"But unless the character of the people is quite different from what it was in my time, you will find that there are difficulties in the way that it will take many years, if not centuries, to overcome.

"You must understand that when we left the United States to come here, it was not a matter of choice, but of necessity. Had we seen a fair prospect of effecting the desired changes, we would not have expatriated ourselves and faced the hardships of a new settlement. But we could see no prospect of a complete change in our time, and only one of gradual but slow improvement."

"Your views are not very encouraging," I said, "and hardly in accord with your belief in evolution, for you must believe in the gradual improvement of society."

"Certainly, I believe in it, and I know that mankind is steadily progressing toward better conditions, and I feel confident that if our institutions are the best calculated to promote happiness and the highest form of civilization, they will be adopted everywhere; for systems of government, as well as public or private institutions, must stand the test of the struggle for existence that the fittest may survive. But the working of this law is exceedingly slow, and under certain conditions centuries may elapse before important changes can be accomplished.

"A change such as you contemplate," he continued, "can only be effected if based upon an increase in the intelligence of the people. I do not believe, Mr. Balcom, that if our institutions could be transplanted bodily in the United States, they would endure for any length of time. Your people are probably ready for some of the changes we have made, and in time may adopt our whole system, but our government is entirely too dependent upon the inner love of order and the good conduct and kindliness of our citizens, to cope with the spirit of greed and individualism which are the marked attributes of the inhabitants of the United States.

"No, unless you can secure a much more intelligent population, one which is fully imbued with the spirit of order and conciliation, one which knows what is the true basis of contentment and happiness, you had better adhere to the existing order of society, improving it as fast as possible, that is as fast as the knowledge of the true conditions of success permeates society.

"Educate the people; educate them not in Greek or Latin, but away from the superstitions which now control their lives; educate them to what is their true position here, to their dependence upon the forces of nature and the absolute necessity of obeying natural laws. Teach them the advantages of co-operation, the beauty of agreement, the vanity and emptiness of show and style, the public danger of the private accumulation of wealth, the folly of dissipation, the waste of quarrels and litigation, and as fast as this education takes hold of the masses, displaces and replaces the old ideas which now control them, so fast, and no faster, will you be able to bring about the changes you are striving for."

Mr. Walter leaned back in his chair in deep thought, and his eyes seemed to take an inward retrospective look. In a moment he raised his head and looking at me said: "Mr. Balcom, our conversation takes me back to those early days when we commenced our settlement. I was a young man then, with more enthusiasm and energy than experience, but many of us were middle-aged or old people, who, tired of strife and competition, were longing for peace and agreement. We were nearly a thousand, men, women and children, and far above the average in knowledge and intelligence. We had left behind us the suspertitious beliefs of the past, and had progressed beyond the follies and weakness of modern civilization.

Our men did not drink or gamble, or spend their time on the streets. Our women did not sacrifice at the shrine of fashion, nor consume their time and strength in foolish attempts to substitute style for comfort. It was the character and the intelligence of these people which enabled them to succeed, and which stamped this young nation with the spirit with which it is animated now, and which underlays and sustains our institutions.

"Had we been quarrelsome, we would have been swamped in the first months of our existence, for new conditions brought to the front many new opinions. Had we been unruly, our simple organization never would have restrained us. Had we been greedy, private ambition would have defeated all our schemes for public welfare.

"But the seed planted by these choice spirits took root and grew. Our children were raised under these influences, and it permeated them thoroughly. Those who joined us later were those who were attracted by a community of desires and ideas, while those among us who became dissatisfied left us to return to other countries.

"It is an axiom in physiology that in a healthy organism the eliminating powers are sufficient to throw off all offensive matter which may be absorbed, and thus the organism be kept in a healthy state. It is just as true in Sociology, and a body economic will drive out naturally all the individuals it cannot control or assimilate, provided always that the influx is not beyond the capacity of its eliminating powers.

"We have ever been mindful of this truth, and while the United States have opened their doors wide to the poor and ignorant of all nations, eager to develop their material resources, and anxious to provide cheap labor for their capitalists, regardless of the difficulty of transforming such persons into intelligent citizens, we have been careful to not encourage emigration, or do anything which would have brought upon us such an outpour as you have received in the United States.

"We are but little known, and do not care to be known. We have no emigration bureau spreading the tidings of our good fortune, and should we ever be threatened with an undesirable emigration, we would not hesitate to prevent it by force if necessary."

"From what you say," I remarked, "I judge that you can give us but little hope of a speedy change, yet surely we must be able to do something to bring about more desirable conditions. We cannot see so much misery and suffering, and know that it can be prevented, and yet fold our hands and passively wait for the good work to accomplish itself. Some one must take measures to enlighten the masses if it is ever to become a reality."

"No, I do not believe that a great deal can be accomplished soon, yet there are many things you can do which would promote the aims you have in view.

"A great deal can be done to educate the people in the true functions of the government, and in the advantages of public co-operation. If you can get the public interested and lead them to study and discuss those questions, a great advance will have been made, and it will open the way for practical experiments.

"But the masses are more easily reached by object lessons than by any other forms of education, and while it is impossible to establish anywhere on American soil an independent Commonwealth like Socioland, you can point out every instance where the principles we advocate have been tried, and emphasize the fact that the results have been uniformely beneficent for the people if honestly conducted. And when this education has been carried long enough to imbue a sufficient

THE CONDITIONS OF SUCCESS. 113

number of persons with these principles, you can gain political control of some city or township, and give the most important features of our system a fair trial.

"Experiments alone can teach what are the conditions that will bring around the desired results, and if a number of persons who have outgrown the present public institutions should find themselves in a position where they could control the public power, and use for their benefit the agencies of public co-operation, their example would be a great educating force, and their influence would slowly radiate until it would affect the whole population.

"The world moves in spite of all conservative influences, and it moves in the right direction. So be of good cheer, and do not feel discouraged because a heavy body like the United States cannot move as fast as our little Commonwealth.

"When you return home you can work in the good cause, and join your efforts to those of the persons who are even now trying to educate the people so as to secure a better form of government. I hope that what you have seen here will help you in your task, and that you will prove a power for good in your native land."

Amen! I say. And may this brief account of what I have seen in this favored Commonwealth induce many to imitate them, and may it be a factor, however humble, in the peaceful evolution of our industrial system, until every person in the land shall receive an adequate share of the comforts that should accrue to all from the progress of civilization.

And now, my dear Harry, while I might write much more that would interest you, I will not extend this account of my visit here, but I will send it to you, that you may reflect on what I have described, and see how it applies to the solution of the problems we are studying.

For my part, I am well satisfied of the superiority of the institutions of Socioland over those of the United States, but I realize fully that the progress they have made is due to the development of their character which enables them to place in the hands of the Commonwealth many of its most important industries, while at the same time they have been able to safely withdraw government control from the departments of morals and religion. The material being better, its cohesive power is greater, and they have been able to erect a much better structure.

For the present, the example of Socioland can only serve us as a beacon to guide our steps, trusting that those who come after us will be able to realize the hope which sustains us in our labors.

Your friend,
Samuel Balcom.

Utopian Literature

AN ARNO PRESS/NEW YORK TIMES COLLECTION

Adams, Frederick Upham.
President John Smith; The Story of a Peaceful Revolution. 1897.

Bird, Arthur.
Looking Forward: A Dream of the United States of the Americas in 1999. 1899.

[Blanchard, Calvin.]
The Art of Real Pleasure. 1864.

Brinsmade, Herman Hine.
Utopia Achieved: A Novel of the Future. 1912.

Caryl, Charles W.
New Era. 1897.

Chavannes, Albert.
The Future Commonwealth. 1892.

Child, William Stanley.
The Legal Revolution of 1902. 1898.

Collens, T. Wharton.
Eden of Labor; or, The Christian Utopia. 1876.

Cowan, James.
Daybreak. A Romance of an Old World. 1896. 2nd ed.

Craig, Alexander.
Ionia; Land of Wise Men and Fair Women. 1898.

Daniel, Charles S.
AI: A Social Vision. 1892.

Devinne, Paul.
The Day of Prosperity: A Vision of the Century to Come. 1902.

Edson, Milan C.
Solaris Farm. 1900.

Fuller, Alvarado M.
A. D. 2000. 1890.

Geissler, Ludwig A.
Looking Beyond. 1891.

Hale, Edward Everett.
How They Lived in Hampton. 1888.

Hale, Edward Everett.
Sybaris and Other Homes. 1869.

Harris, W. S.
Life in a Thousand Worlds. 1905.

Henry, W. O.
Equitania. 1914.

Hicks, Granville, with Richard M. Bennett.
The First to Awaken. 1940.

Lewis, Arthur O., editor
American Utopias: Selected Short Fiction. 1790–1954.

McGrady, Thomas.
Beyond the Black Ocean. 1901.

Mendes H. Pereira.
Looking Ahead. 1899.

Michaelis, Richard.
Looking Further Forward. An Answer to *Looking Backward* by Edward Bellamy. 1890.

Moore, David A.
The Age of Progress. 1856.

Noto, Cosimo.
The Ideal City. 1903.

Olerich, Henry.
A Cityless and Countryless World. 1893.

Parry, David M.
The Scarlet Empire. 1906.

Peck, Bradford.
The World a Department Store. 1900.

Reitmeister, Louis Aaron.
If Tomorrow Comes. 1934.

Roberts, J. W.
Looking Within. 1893.

Rosewater, Frank.
'96; A Romance of Utopia. 1894.

Satterlee, W. W.
Looking Backward and What I Saw. 2nd ed. 1890.

Schindler, Solomon.
Young West; A Sequel to Edward Bellamy's Celebrated Novel "Looking Backward." 1894.

Smith, Titus K.
Altruria. 1895.

Steere, C. A.
When Things Were Doing. 1908.

Taylor, William Alexander.
Intermere. 1901.

Thiusen, Ismar.
The Diothas, or, A Far Look Ahead. 1883.

Vinton, Arthur Dudley.
Looking Further Backward. 1890.

Wooldridge, C. W.
Perfecting the Earth. 1902.

Wright, Austin Tappan.
Islandia. 1942.